How to Flirt

A Practical Guide
• • • • • • • • • • • • •
Marty Westerman

Illustrations by Stephanie Donon

PRICE STERN SLOAN, INC.
A MEMBER OF
THE PUTNAM BERKLEY GROUP, INC.
NEW YORK

ACKNOWLEDGMENTS

Every book is a marvelous team effort. This is my first book, and I thank the members of my "First Team": Eddie Westerman—reader, designer, CreativeDater and life partner; Yona & Nate Kellman, and Arne & Claire Westerman—our parents and best salespeople; Wendy Katz—friend and PageMaker Goddess; Dan Kennedy—friend, ideaman and marketer extraordinaire; Jane Bryant, who said, "Write a book!"; friends Matthew Monroe, Tom Hebert, Dan Gilbert, Joyce Stanton and Elizabeth Wales; Guy Cournoyer at U. District Kinko's; Dana Boyer and Lee Soper at University of Washington Bookstore; Jutta at Elliott Bay Books; Barbara Bailey at Bailey-Coy Books; Kim at Love Pantry; Karen Kummerfeldt at LoveSeason; Greg Coe at America's #1 jazz station, KPLU; and all those flirtatious folks who helped make this enterprise possible.

DEDICATION

To my patron and wife, Edna Kellman Westerman. What can I fix you for lunch tomorrow?

Copyright © 1992 by Marty Westerman

Published by Price Stern Sloan, Inc.
a member of
The Putnam Berkley Group, Inc.
200 Madison Avenue
New York, NY 10016

10 9 8 7 6 5

Library of Congress Cataloging-in-Publication Data

Westerman, Marty
    How to flirt/Marty Westerman
        p. cm.
    ISBN 0-8431-3380-5
        1. Man-woman relationships. 2. Interpersonal attraction.
    3. Etiquette. I. Title.
    HQ801.W64   1992
    646.7'7—dc   2092-15958
                                                          CIP

NOTICE: The information contained in this book is true and complete to the best of our knowledge. All recommendations are made without any guarantees on the part of the author or of Price Stern Sloan, Inc. The author and publisher disclaim all liability in connection with the use of this information.

DISCLAIMER: This book is intended to amuse, provoke and entertain our kind readers. It offers the fruits of "Dr. Flirt's" experience and research over the years, with which our reading friends may do as they wish. "Dr. Flirt" can only assume responsibility for his own actions, not for those of our gentle readers. "Dr. Flirt" is a nickname, along with "Flirtmaster," "Flirtmeister" and "The Flirtster," all of which have been applied to the author. He is not a real doctor (PhD, JD, MD or ND).

Table of Contents

Introduction

Everybody has some idea what flirting is—comments with a naughty edge, right? Wrong. On the subject of *flirting*, the *new* flirting, I could fill a book (which I have, you'll notice). Sure, it's a glance across a crowded room, a light touch, a friendly comment. But you can also flirt with a bag of potato chips, a business card or a dog. Wait a minute. I couldn't help noticing, but you look just like (choose one):

- ☐ William Hurt
- ☐ Michelle Pfeiffer
- ☐ Dustin Hoffman
- ☐ Julia Roberts
- ☐ Kevin Costner
- ☐ Cher
- ☐ my college roommate

You can flirt with anybody, anywhere, anytime—with props or without. Yet, most people are sure they're doing this flirting thing "wrong," because sometimes people they approach ignore them, or say, "No, I'm not interested." So they don't do it at all. Give this a try: Wow, (choose another):

- ☐ what beautiful earrings!
- ☐ that was a brilliant answer!
- ☐ nice boots/garden/terminal/car/studio!
- ☐ how do you stay in such good shape?

Not flirting is a mistake because, frankly, it's a lot of fun. Say, didn't I see you at (your choice):

- ☐ the art gallery tour Thursday?
- ☐ the grocery store?
- ☐ that town meeting last week?
- ☐ the yacht club?
- ☐ the mall?
- ☐ *Les Misérables* in San Francisco?

That's the reason for this book. Flirting can be as easy as playing checkers with your grandad or as complex as modern dance. Either way it's a good time. You don't have to be a "natural." You can't be. Even the people you think are great at flirting had to learn how to do it. And if they can, you can, too. All you have to do is go out and use your imagination.

1

•••••

OLD WORLD CHARM

First, I'll clear up a misconception about flirting. Flirting *is not* leading people on, or combing the night spots for love. That is called *hunting*—a high-pressure pursuit that uses very different techniques: revealing clothes; lots of scent; excessive flattery; conspicuous lip licking, hip rolling and ogling; running fingers down wineglass stems while staring fixedly at the prospect; lascivious eating or drinking; running a toe up your prospect's leg; or cat-stretching full length with arms extended. It includes lines like, "I wanna meet you, baby, and I mean M-E-A-T," "Wanna party?" and "I not only respect you now, I'll respect you in the morning."

None of these is flirting, friends.

Flirting is pressure-free. You can do it night or day, with anyone, anywhere. You don't need the right clothes. It's a playful bit of attention you give somebody, or they give you. I recall an old Czech proverb, "Do not protect yourself by a fence, but rather by your friends." That's the objective of flirting. The successful flirt has lots of friends. The successful hunter has trophies.

Let's clear up a second misconception about flirting too: single adults are *not* the only people who do it. Most often, flirting *does not* occur with a love interest, or have a "naughty" edge.

You may think of Romeo and Juliet. But also think of children with big eyes and unexpected smiles that melt your heart; parents who tell you on prom night that you're the most beautiful or handsome kid in town; and shopkeepers, colleagues and strangers who banter or unexpectedly toss you the odd compliment or silly question.

Nobody puts their ego on the line flirting. Whether you're married, single, young, old, male or female, you can flirt—anywhere, with anyone, at any time. Flirting is a family value.

THE FIRST RULE OF FLIRTING
Make yourself, and somebody else, feel special.

In flirting, everybody comes away feeling good about themselves.

I was on a talk show once where the host said, "I just want my wife to know I don't flirt."

"No," I said, "you still flirt. That's what makes you a good host. You just don't hunt."

Hey, maybe he *doesn't* flirt with his wife. But he should.

Flirting is a necessary skill today.

If you're single, you've probably found the safest motto to live by in the 90s is, "Date, don't mate." Flirting is the way you get to know the person *before* you go to bed with them. In fact, it may be the way you decide *not* to.

Whether you're single or not, you probably see more people in one week than your rural grandparents saw in a year, or a lifetime (Really! See Alvin Tofler's book, *Future Shock*).

Also, wherever you work, live and play, you want and need information to get ahead, learn about opportunities and just make your life better. The people around you have that information, and they will share it with you for your mutual benefit—*if* you make them feel good about it. Flirting is your key to interacting with all these folks, and to getting that information.

Finally, on your social scene, when you couple flirting with CreativeDating (see chapter 7), it helps give dimension to every relationship from your first date to your successful marriage.

Flirting, friends, is the art of being disarming. It enables you to pass whole through people's defenses and make them smile.

Now supposedly, men are much less likely to notice flirting behavior than women. I've never seen any research, however, to prove it. Studies do show that men are less likely to notice and talk about personal details (see chapter 5). So hey, if you're ever unsure about whether or not that other person is flirting, ask: "Are you flirting with me?"

Many people flirt while going about trivial daily chores.

They flirt on the phone, regardless of what sex the other person is. They flirt by mail and on their computer terminals.

You can flirt for years with your spouse, significant other or favorite family member. You can flirt with friends, people at the office or school, and to make new business contacts. You can do it in elevators, on buses, at weddings, funerals and bar mitzvahs. You can even do it for a moment with a stranger—say, with street vendors when you pick up a hot dog or newspaper.

Some people think you need "chemistry" to flirt. It's nice to have, but is it chemistry when you play peek-a-boo with a baby? Is it naughty when you walk into a store where the shopkeeper or salesclerk says, "My, you are looking well today! And that's a beautiful/handsome (purse, dog, baby, boy, girl, jacket, hat)! So, how may I help you?"

That's just plain good sales technique.

Some people call this "laying it on thick." I call it "Old World Charm." Even if you call it "the niceties" or "small talk," there isn't enough of it around anymore.

Those clerks and vendors are flirting with you—encouraging you to feel welcome, comfortable, special. They use eye contact, voice, smile, body language, all to draw you toward themselves and their products. Good waitpeople at bars and restaurants do the same things. They give eye contact, smiles and prompt service. You feel special and pay them back with good tips.

Who would you rather dance with: The person who comes up to you and says, "I've been looking at that great (haircut, shirt, jacket, pair of boots, etc.) of yours, and wondered where you got it?" and then asks for a dance? Or the person who comes up and grumbles, "Wanna dance?"

We're not talking chemistry here. We're talking *skill*.

"Flirting," says an elderly woman friend of mine, "makes people feel good."

Some years ago, her daughter, a flight attendant, won a free trip to Rome and took her along. "We were sitting in a café," recalled my friend, "and a waiter came up to me and said, 'I want to compliment you on your beautiful child, and I wonder if I could have the honor of her going out with me? I will bring my parents to meet you.'"

"Well," said my friend, "what mother doesn't want to be complimented on her child? He did bring his parents, and we went out to lunch. We enjoyed ourselves so much in Italy, we stayed longer than the free prize period, but when I went to pay the hotel bill, the desk clerk said, 'No madam, we wouldn't dream of taking your money, since you have a daughter who won a beauty contest in America.' I tried to explain, but he wouldn't hear of it. 'No,' he said, 'you are being too modest.'"

Recently, my father-in-law was accosted by a young woman who had just come from China on tour. She asked directions, and then added, "Is there any danger walking around here?" He replied, "The only danger is that some young man will fall in love with you and marry you, and you won't want to go home."

My older woman friend has lamented that, "Flirting is not as successful now as it was back in the '40s. There were two kinds of girls, good girls (virgins) and bad girls (non-virgins). If you were good, you could say anything and nobody would misunderstand you. You could be perfectly outrageous and still have fun."

Well, I have good news folks: *people haven't changed.*

We still expect certain people to flirt, and certain people not to. There are things we each accept as appropriate from some people, and not from others. And some of us see ourselves as flirtatious, some of us don't. It's just like old times.

So look at this new flirting as an opportunity to try out new things, to step outside your preconceptions and expectations! You'll have some successes, you'll have some "learning experiences" and you'll become a skilled practitioner of the art of flirting.

THE ZERO-DEFECT LAW OF FLIRTING
Nobody "fails" or "makes mistakes" when flirting. They just try things and learn from them.

Now, everyone can probably tell some embarrassing flirting or dating stories. The key thing is to transform each "failure" into a "learning opportunity" through the miracle of fresh perspective.

Humans start getting embarrassed as early as the age of five, when we first become self-aware, says Dr. Edward Gross, a University of Washington sociology professor. He believes that nature "would not have played such a dirty trick on us," that is, given us the capacity to get embarrassed, if it didn't serve some important human function, such as signaling for help or forgiveness, or stopping us from carrying on with something foolish.

Most embarrassment results from getting ourselves exposed in public, or from fearing exposure. In the grand scheme, embarrassment is one of the great weapons the American news media has for keeping our governments and other powerful organizations and people in check. In the small scheme of things, which is our milieu for this book, we all know that embarrassments make good stories later, after we have put the events in perspective.

Dr. Gross has distilled four techniques for achieving that transformation of perspective—from one of personal failure to one of personal accomplishment. They include:

1. prevent embarrassing event(s) from happening

2. reduce their significance

3. change the meaning of what happened

4. pretend you weren't yourself when it happened

Q: How is that done in practice, Dr. Flirt?

A: Usually, you don't expect embarrassing events to occur (except on television shows such as "Candid Camera" and "America's Funniest Videos"). But, they happen. Then, you have the opportunity to prevent their happening again. Here are some examples:

A biologist friend of mine once picked up the phone to call friends for a chat. He routinely plays games with telephone numbers, and he remembered theirs by recalling that it added up to 9-11-11-11. So, he absent-mindedly dialed that, and within seconds, the police were at his door. He used techniques (2) and (3): "Boy," he told the officers apologetically, "I wish my friends would show up this fast when I call!" He now uses technique (1), and looks up phone numbers before he dials.

President Bush has achieved a unique place as the only head of state in recorded history to vomit in the lap of another head of state. Bush's medical advisor warned the ill leader away from attending the dinner, but Bush ignored him. In the future, Bush will use techniques (1) and (4). His predecessor, Ronald Reagan, used technique (4) all the time.

You may know somebody who is vain about wearing glasses. I knew such a fellow when I was in the Coast Guard. One night, he went out with the boys and refused to wear his glasses. At one bar, he wanted to dance, so he walked over to a beautiful head of long blonde hair and popped the question. The head turned around and there was a beautiful long blonde beard on the other side. My buddy backpedaled with technique (4)—"Sorry! I'm not wearing my glasses!"—and with distance from the event, has (2) reduced its significance. He does technique (1) now, by wearing glasses or contacts wherever he goes.

One of the all-time funniest CreativeDates (see chapter 7) happened to a friend of mine one February a few years ago. A cheerful outdoorsman, he decided to make his first date with a new woman special. After dinner, he took her for a canoe ride and dessert on the lake in Seattle's most-popular city park. They both dressed for the cool weather. He paddled them out to the middle of the lake, and they picnicked romantically by candle light, facing each other across the canoe's center seat.

When they were ready to head for shore, she stood up to turn and face the bow. It was her first time in a canoe, and they went right over. It took the better part of the next hour to get themselves and the boat out of the chilly water, and by the time they could call an aid car for the hospital, they had hypothermia. It was two in the morning before the hospital decided they were warm enough to be released. His car was back at the lake, so he called his housemate for a ride home. His date was still shivering from remembered terror, and she spent the night at his place, bundled in blankets on the couch.

But as early as a week later, our friend was able to laugh about this experience, by employing techniques (1) and (3). Now, he explains canoe procedures to inexperienced people; he takes lifejackets and does the lake in warmer weather.

MORE THAN TALK

Lest you think that flirting is all talk, I remind you that it can also be silent (a wink or smile) or physical (a light touch). Eye contact, smiling and raising eyebrows are recognized as greeting signs in cultures worldwide.

To flirt, you don't have to make voice contact at all, which is good news for people who feel uncomfortable making "the first move." You can just make one "move" and go your merry way. You don't have to set up a chase and catch anyone, though that's fun (see chapters 2 and 5), nor let anyone catch you.

I recall a female friend of mine who found one of her housemates watching television one evening. She planned to throw a party at her group house, and, courteously, she told the housemate, "Feel free to invite any friends you want."

He raised his arm and pointed at the TV. "These are my friends," he said.

Flirting is an ideal pursuit for shy people. You can do it in front of a mirror. Or you can do it in public as a total no-contact sport. Each *flirt* only takes a few seconds. I'll show you:

THE COMPLETE LIST OF PROVEN FLIRTING TECHNIQUES

TECHNIQUE	TIME
Acknowledging someone (nod, wave, etc.)	1-2 seconds
Asking a question	1-4 seconds
Batting eyelashes	0.4 seconds
Beckoning (finger, hand)	1-3 seconds
Being patient	forever!
Begging	3 excruciating seconds
Cocking head	2 seconds
Complimenting someone	4-8 seconds
Crying	4-8 seconds
Dropping handkerchief, tissue	2 seconds
Dropping books, papers	3 seconds
Flaring nostrils	0.7 seconds
"Flashing" an item (fancy car, flowers, AmEx card, stuffed animal)	1-6 seconds
Flirting with someone to get a third party's attention	5-10 seconds
Fluttering fan	1.5 seconds
Flying paper airplane	2 seconds
Following prospect around	5-6 minutes
Fondling produce in grocery store	4-12 seconds
Hitching up pants, skirt; checking stockings, hat, buckles, etc.	2 seconds
Honking horn	1-2 seconds
Laying coat across puddle	4 seconds
Lighting candle or incense for prospect	7 seconds

TECHNIQUE	TIME
Blowing out match without pregnant pause	0.8 seconds
Blowing out match with pregnant pause	4.2 seconds
Looking over tops of eye- or sunglasses	1.6 seconds
Making a face	1.3 seconds
Making eye contact	0.5 seconds
Offering help	2-8 seconds
One-liner delivery	2.3 seconds
Opening door, pulling chair out, helping with coat	2-5 seconds
Overtipping at restaurants	2 seconds
Panting obviously, drooling	2-4 seconds
Pulling your shirt open	2 seconds
Playing with tie, earring, hair, jewelry, etc.	2-5 seconds
Pulling prospect's hair	1.5 seconds
Raising eyebrows	0.3 seconds
Raising glass in salute	2 seconds
Sending card, drink	8-90 seconds
Shaking hands, extra squeeze	3.8 seconds
Smiling (plain, conspiratorial or "come-hither")	1-3 seconds
Telling joke, making quip	2-10 seconds
Tipping hat	0.3 seconds
Touching lightly (on hand, wrist or forearm)	4 seconds *maximum*
Waving handkerchief, tissue	4 seconds
Whistling	1.2 seconds
Winking (plain or conspiratorial)	0.5 seconds
Wrinkling nose	0.5 seconds
Writing and sending a note	20-50 seconds

You can do each technique alone or combine them, for example: wrinkling nose + raising eyebrows, simultaneously. Not all these techniques may be for you, of course. Use only what you feel comfortable using.

We people with good eyesight almost always make eye contact when we flirt. But how do sight-impaired people flirt? By voice and touch. Hearing-impaired people? By eye contact and touch.

Obviously, you don't need to learn formulas or one-liners for meeting people. As my neighborhood nurseryman says, "This isn't brain surgery." You don't even need courage. Just refer to The Complete List. It's got everything you need to make the first move. You'll find how to make the second move, of course, in chapter 2.

Now it's time for your first exercise.

Flirting is a skill. It takes practice to master, but oh, the rewards! Once you've learned to flirt, you can meet and get comfortable with almost anybody you choose.

FLIRT EXERCISE #1
Pay a compliment.

Look up from this book. Locate someone near you. Think of a compliment you can give them. Don't say anything, just think of one.

I can hear you now.

"That's it?" you demand. "Nice hat?!"

Yes, that's it. "Nice hat." You're already flirting.

Most people don't believe it's that simple. A lot of articles and books will have you believe that men and women are mysterious adversaries, even enemies, and they need complex scripts and behavior plans to make contact.

No way.

Men and women *do* have different expectations and make different conversations (more on that in chapters 4, 5 and 6).

But everybody loves a compliment, and enjoys cheer. That's all there is to good flirting.

Before I started to teach a flirt class one evening, a woman took me aside. "Can you make me an expert in one-liners tonight?" she whispered.

"Do you use them in real life?" I asked.

"No," she said.

"Then I can't. One-liners are not you. Just be yourself and you'll meet all the people you want." No doubt, after that class she went on to become the wealthy, celebrated and happy person she is today.

My point is:

THE SECOND RULE OF FLIRTING

Flirt where you are comfortable.

Flirt who you are.

How to select comfortable places for you is described in chapter 4.

How you *be* yourself is up to you. The first question is, do you like what *yourself* is? Try this next exercise. Remember: if you like yourself, then you can be certain other people will like you, too. And hey—fill in *all 12* blanks.

FLIRT EXERCISE #2

The Dozen Things I Like About Myself:

1. _____
2. _____
3. _____
4. _____
5. _____
6. _____
7. _____
8. _____
9. _____
10. _____
11. _____
12. _____

By the way, as Dr. Flirt, I expect you to carry this book with you. Showing the cover is a great way to flirt. Using what's inside is even better.

And remember: never flirt if you think you *should* be flirting. If you ever catch yourself thinking, "I should get out and flirt!" or "I should be able to flirt with that person!" ask yourself, "Why?" Both these "shoulds" violate The Second Rule of Flirting.

Flirt when you *want* to, in places where you're comfortable and with people you believe have things in common with you.

THE TRUST THING

Being disarming, and getting through somebody's defenses, means winning their *trust*. When you flirt with people, they open up to you, and that gives you a responsibility to be honest with them. As my father says, "Use this for good, and not for evil." Flirting should be sincere, whether you use it to crash a party, charm your way past an administrative assistant or win a child's heart.

The smart folks in the business world view trust as a *product*. For example, Bill Totten, president of the Japanese software firm Ashisuto K.K., *does not* want his salespeople relentlessly hunting customers to meet sales and dollar quotas. Instead, he expects them to develop personal relationships with customers through frequent calls and visits.

Working this way over the long term, they bring in a lot of business, says Totten, "because most customers prefer to buy from people they know, and like and trust." Totten asserts that providing excellent service to existing customers makes them the best prospects to buy additional products. In fact, nearly 75% of Ashisuto's trade is the result of repeat-business accounts.

Totten has noted that even in business there is a difference between *flirting* and *hunting*. It is the same in social interaction. Most people prefer to become friends with people they know, like and trust. More on the business side in chapter 6.

Now, dictionaries and thesauri define flirting in generally negative or sexual terms, though *we* know from doing it quite the contrary. Flirting is a lot of good, clean, light, playful fun.

Rest assured friends, in this book, Dr. Flirt emphasizes *the positive*.

The True Meaning of Flirting

Webster's New World Dictionary of the American Language says our word, "flirt," is both a verb and a noun that dates from a 16th century old French word having to do with a giddy girl, touching lightly and moving from flower to flower.

Webster's current definitions include: to move or wave quickly (as, the bird *flirted* its tail), to reflect on something without serious intentions (as, he *flirted* with the idea of quitting his job) and a person who plays at love.

Webster also lists *coquet* (pronounced ko-ket in English) as a synonym to flirt. This unflattering word describes "the behavior of a flirtatious woman who promiscuously seeks attention or admiration without serious intent." This is *hunting*, friends. It's what gold diggers, hussies, gigilos, mashers and wolves do.

Our flirting doesn't involve serious kissing, caressing, ogling or hustling. Ours is coy. It can involve glances, light touching and hugging, blowing a kiss and gentle patting, but none of these are necessary to most flirting.

Roget's Thesaurus says that to flirt is "to dally, linger" and "be idle," among other things. It's something to do when you feel relaxed and comfortable. Roget may take this view because he's French. Webster is a puritanistic American.

That brings up an interesting point. Americans always complain they don't have enough time to do what they want to do. They tend to always feel rushed, which may be why they do more hunting than flirting.

Georgia Witkin confirms this complaint in *The Female Stress Syndrome* (Newmarket). Between work and home activities, she says, women don't take enough time out for themselves every day. Yet, all they need for mental health, she calculates, is 21 minutes a day, in a block or segments. And I believe this applies just as much, or more, to men.

So, take out some time for yourself every day and flirt. You can do every technique on the Complete List in *less than six minutes*.

There's another definition to flirting, too. You have probably seen it in action at bars, political functions and big parties. The "networking" folk—politicians, organizers, hosts, hostesses and people who want to feel important—"work the crowd." They shake hands, ask a question, chat and generally make certain that (1) things are running smoothly, and (2) they are getting their faces and cards passed around. This is also called "schmoozing" and "brown-nosing," depending upon the circumstances.

At worst, as practiced at Hollywood and other networking parties, it is a parasitic and often dishonest pursuit in which each schmoozer hunts the person or people who can advance his or her career.

At best, however, it is a warm skill, and the practitioners are surprisingly adept at convincing dozens, maybe hundreds of people in a short time that they have each been given a little friendly attention.

As you can see, we North Americans tend to give flirting a positive or negative spin depending on its context. Dr. Flirt asks that you broaden your definition to create a clear distinction between flirting, which is warm and playful, and hunting, which isn't.

With that in mind, let's take a fast trip through time and across the seas, where, according to this item edited from the Reuters News Service Wire, the Turks have yet to broaden their sense of flirting:

> *Istanbul [Reuters] 11/15/90—A Muslem fundamentalist minister in the Turkish cabinet asserted Thursday that flirting is no different from prostitution. When questioned, State Family Development Minister Cimel Cicek replied he meant flirting which leads to unlawful sexual relations, specifically, pre-marital relations.*
>
> *"It is always the woman who loses in flirting," he said.*
>
> *In response, the Turkish opposition Socialist Party has protested and asked that he resign after his "demeaning words against women." Turkish actress Lale Oraloglu demanded, "If he calls a flirting woman a prostitute, what will he call a man who flirts?" An Istanbul University Professor, Coskun Ozdemir, remarked, "It is dismaying to see a state minister so far behind the times and the world."*

In this book, we view flirting as a way to perk things up, start conversations and actions, kill boredom and provide some fun. You can use it to test how outgoing you feel, to pay someone attention, or to enjoy as a way others pay attention to you.

2
•••••

HOW MUCH FUN CAN YOU HAVE?

"**T**his is great information, Dr. Flirt, but where do I get the courage to just go out and, well, talk to people? I don't want to sound stupid."

Dr. Flirt suggests you put social contact in perspective.

....
THE THIRD RULE OF FLIRTING
Keep your sense of humor. Don't take yourself too seriously.
....

I was surprised the first time somebody asked about courage. It was a woman who had spent an entire afternoon at a huge garden party, repeatedly catching the eye of an attractive man. He would smile back, but they were both working the crowd (since it was a fund-raising event), and they kept passing without contact.

"Passing" is the key word here. She did it on purpose, she finally admitted, because she couldn't work up the courage to cut through that crowd and give him her card until the end of the afternoon. By then, he was gone.

A designer friend of mine, who was on the set of a popular television show, was asked to leave just before filming started. On her way out, she passed the show's handsome male star, who was on his way in. "I'm sorry," he said to her, "but you make me nervous."

She was attracted to this guy and asked if she should pursue him. "Sure," I said. "Find out if he means nervous *good* or nervous *bad*. Send him a note."

"Well, I'm not sure he'll remember me," she allowed sheepishly. "This happened a month ago." Dr. Flirt's advice: forget it. The trail is cold now.

Women aren't the only flirt procrastinators.

A man from one of my seminars was at his health club one morning, doing a stationary bicycle workout, when an attractive woman walked into the room. "She had five bikes to choose from," the man told me, "but she chose the one right next to mine. We pedaled for 15 minutes and didn't say a word. Then she got up and left. I couldn't think of a thing to say."

"How about, 'Wanna race?'" I suggested. I mean, how can somebody go for 15 minutes, or even one minute, without saying anything?

"I didn't want to say anything stupid," he answered.

FLIRT PSYCHOLOGY 101
You are the only person who can
make *you* feel stupid.

It's true. Think of it as a talent. Nobody else on earth can do it. Other people can help. They can laugh, they can sneer, they can say whatever they want. That's them—not you. Remember the old "sticks and stones" rhyme? *You* are the one in control, the one who can believe in yourself and make what you want happen. And as long as we're talking about talent, try this on for size:

FLIRT PSYCHOLOGY 102
You are the only person who can
make *you* feel great.

It's true. Think of it as a talent, just like you did in Flirt Psychology 101.

This may be news to you, but with few exceptions, such as a chemical imbalance in the body, each of us can control our emotions and reprogram our reactions to certain things.

I think of that old Scottish proverb: "Be happy while you're living, for you're a long time dead."

The techniques for building self-esteem fall under the heading of "behavior modification," which involves teaching people healthy new ways to deal with old problems and challenges. About 33,000 studies of human behavior are done annually around the world, and publishers bring out dozens of "behavior mod" books each year.

There are also thousands of therapists, social workers, psychologists, psychotherapists, bodyworkers, psychiatrists and other mental health professionals and groups (from AA and The Forum to Silva and Weight Watchers), that are in the business of showing people how they can take control of their lives.

All of which lies outside the scope of this book. As you'll recall, this one is about flirting.

But just for fun, I'll tease you with an exercise (see Q & A, p. 21-22).

There's a Gestalt psychology theory that claims we can modify our emotional reactions to stimuli by viewing our "emotions" as interpretations of our *physical* reactions to different stimuli. Our muscles only do two things: relax and contract. Yet, humans use amazing imagination to interpret these two muscle actions.

For example, relaxed muscles are interpreted as happy, self-confident, loving, victorious, sleepy and/or satisfied. Tense muscles are fearful, hateful, angry, anxious, and/or engaged in work or sport. Now, the exercise:

....

FLIRT EXERCISE #3
Test your reflexes.

....

Next time you have an emotion, stop and sense what your muscles are doing (relaxing or contracting?) and which ones are doing it. That's what your emotion is, physically. Try playing with the muscles. Can you relax the tense ones, and tense the relaxed ones? See if your emotion changes. If nothing else, this exercise will distract you for a moment.

To learn more about this, head for your library, or look in the Yellow Pages® under "P" (psychologists, psychiatrists, etc.) or "T" (therapists). They'll be happy to make appointments with you to explain and expand on this information.

Meanwhile, I'll stick to flirting, a light-hearted pursuit, and avoid violating The Third Rule of Flirting (don't take yourself too seriously)!

Most Americans, however, tend to take themselves *very seriously*, and for that reason, say my European friends, Americans find it hard to flirt.

Playfulness goes against the grain of the Puritan Work Ethic (PWE). I mean, can you picture a Puritan, in black hat, frock coat and buckle shoes, doing stand-up comedy? Or a bunch of Puritans playing touch football, or hanging out at a sidewalk café drinking java? The old PWE kills playful impulses, friends. We must break through it to achieve good, colorful flirting.

Look, for a moment, at Europe: bastion of the Catholic, Calvinist, Lutheran, Greek Orthodox and Anglican Churches; ravaged by wars for 2,000 years; a continent where countless political, financial and industrial empires and tyrants have ascended and crashed, yet—*they still flirt.*

Sit in any café today, from Lisbon, Portugal, to Tel Aviv, Israel, to Oslo, Norway, and you'll see the eyes flash and smiles traded. Drop into a Dublin, Ireland, greengrocer's or a Lucerne, Switzerland, clothing store, and the shopkeepers will greet you with a smile and a compliment. Long before there was an America, even before there was a Europe, people on the continent were flirting, and people in China were peeking over open fans (see chapter 3).

Yes, even in the midst of disasters, these people kept their senses of humor. It's the key to survival, and to flirting. That's why we Americans invented Murphy's Laws (see *The Complete Murphy's Law*, Price Stern Sloan) and all the other jokes that go with just getting through each day.

So, how many of you *don't* have a sense of humor? You can test this easily.

··

THE OFFICIAL FLIRTING HUMOR TEST

	YES	NO
Have you ever laughed?	☐	☐

··

If you answered yes to this question, you have a sense of humor. Maybe you don't think it's appropriate to joke. Maybe you think other people aren't funny. But, most importantly, *you can laugh.*

The key to flirting is being playful. The key to playfulness, to having a good time, is a sense of humor. You can create magic. It doesn't just happen, you know. You create it out of a good frame of mind, when you are in situations that you enjoy, with people you enjoy. Take a few minutes now to jot down a list of things that put you in a good frame of mind.

FLIRT EXERCISE #4
THE DOZEN THINGS THAT MAKE ME FEEL GOOD

1. _____

2. _____

3. _____

4. _____

5. _____

6. _____

7. _____

8. _____

9. _____

10. _____

11. _____

12. _____

Fill in the whole list. It can be as simple as watching flowers bloom, getting letters in the mail, or celebrating a win by your favorite sports team. It can be as complex as solving a problem, singing with a jazz band, or the moment of birthing a baby.

Think too, on what builds your confidence. What do you do for yourself, and what do others do for or with you, that makes you feel strong and good inside?

When you feel good about yourself, the sense of humor comes right along. You can talk to anybody and say anything you like.

Here's a way to practice:

Next time you phone a bank, insurance company or airline reservations agent, as you wait for the person to find your information, talk with them. If it's an airline, the agent is most likely far away, so you're getting a long distance call and conversation for free. Ask where they are. How's the weather there? Do you fly to Nairobi? How about if you're talking with the bank—will they lend you money to open a petting zoo? And how about the insurance broker? Will the company cover your shoelace collection, or insure your bungee jumping team?

Either the person on the other end will respond, or they won't. They can't *see* you. So you're safe to say *anything* without feeling embarrassed. You'll never see this person, anyway.

If the person responds, enjoy it. For a few moments, you "take" to each other and have fun feeling the conversation moving, like a leaf drifting down a stream, or if you're really hitting it off—it's as if you're river rafting down whitewater. However it goes, finish the conversation and go your merry way. My mother in law does this all the time. She is an active officer in women's clubs, and every day she charms people on the phone and in person. And she gets results: excellent service, better prices on tickets, tours and other activities, and helpful favors for the women's clubs, her friends and herself.

In your phone conversation, *do not ask for a date*. Just enjoy an exhilarating chat and know you are building your confidence for flirting.

My European friends also complain that, "Americans can't take compliments."

A Dutch furniture-maker friend once grumbled, "Europeans take compliments very well. They seem more comfortable with themselves, with their place in the scheme of things. But Americans, they put all this effort into their appearances. They spend time on their houses and gardens and vehicles, but when someone notices and compliments them, they say, 'Oh, it's nothing. Or, it's not that great.' All they have to say is, 'Thank you.'"

FLIRT EXERCISE #6
Accept a compliment.

Look up from this book. Find somebody to give you a compliment. Show them this book and tell them what you are doing. It's important! Then say, "Thank you." Not, "Oh, it's nothing special." Just, "Thank you." Practice basking in the warmth of appreciation. You deserve it.

As you can see, whether you make contact or not, it takes two to flirt: a flirt*er* and a flirt*ee*.

The flirt*er* takes the initiative (i.e., a raised eyebrow) and the flirt*ee* responds (i.e., eyebrow, wink or smile). As things develop, the flirter switches roles back and forth with the flirtee. That can happen for you every time, after you've mastered the information in this book.

A person can sit before a mirror and do no-contact flirting (see Complete List of Proven Flirting Techniques) 'til the cows come home. But long before the cows show up, I'll bet even a terribly shy person would get impatient. It's like trying to play a game of tag by yourself.

So if you are a person who *does* want to make some sort of contact, you learn the skill of flirting. Plain and simple. You add art to that flirting from your own vivid imagination and personality. Contact flirting lessons begin in chapter 4.

Flirting isn't like going to work, where you are obligated to show up and do it, no matter what. It's a leisure activity. You *can* do it at work. But no matter where you do it, if you want to project that playfulness so necessary to flirting, you must feel good.

Q: Do I have to be "in the mood" to flirt?

A: Generally, yes. This doesn't mean you have to be inspired to flirt, although that's always helpful. But a good frame of mind is important. To help, review your Flirt Exercises #1, #2, #3 and #4. When you feel positive or inspired, give youself the green light to flirt. When you don't, don't. It's that simple. You can always supplement the exercises by watching cartoons, by reading a funny book, seeing a funny movie or by talking with somebody you really enjoy.

Q: Can I hide my mood?

A: Sure you can. You can pretend you feel better than you do (which sometimes makes you *actually* feel better, or which sometimes backfires if you are pressuring yourself into something you don't want to do). Basically, your mood is up to you.

The word "person" comes from the Latin *persona*, a face mask worn by actors. This explains why people "take you at face value." But people also "give character." That's how folks in parts of southern and western United States describe flirting. In other words, they decide to see you in a particular way, and to them, that's who you are, whether you agree or not.

Bummer. Research done in England shows that you have two to four *minutes* to make a first impression, whether it's for flirting, a job interview or business deal. And it's difficult to change a person's mind about that impression afterward.

It explains why actors who are known for a certain part find it so hard to break into other roles. Musicians have the same difficulty "crossing over" to other styles. Their audiences want to keep them in the old roles, where they're familiar.

That's also one of the reasons you may find it hard to change your own habits. After you've made the shift, the people around you know and support you as your old self. You've got to retrain them to support you as the new person you've become. But I digress.

Q: You mean I can actually change my mood on the spot? And change the moods of people around me, too?

A: Yes, apparently. Studies at the University of Michigan, Clark University in Worcester, Massachusetts, and the University of California San Francisco Medical School, showed that: 1) as you relax and contract facial muscles, you change the temperature and flow of blood to the brain centers that regulate emotions; 2) your facial expressions can arouse moods in yourself and other people, and 3) people who mimic emotions can cause changes in their body temperatures and breath rates, and bring on psychological reactions.

Basically, these are the things that actors do.

Some people hide their moods or shyness by dressing up in costume—for parties, games, Halloween, Mardi Gras, Purim or the theater. A woman in one of my flirt classes said a costume made her feel like a different person. "I felt so free!" she said. "I wish I could be that way in real life!"

What this woman didn't realize is, that costume *is* real life. Another *persona*.

Each of us plays several roles every day. We are one person at work, another person at home. We are different alone than with friends, our significant other or children. We're different again at our place of worship and on vacation. Travel to a new place, and *boom!* nobody knows you, so you can be anybody you want. Just as it is when you're on the telephone. Who needs a costume? The trick is to teach yourself how you can carry that free attitude wherever you are.

People have told me, "Gosh, Dr. Flirt, I don't have that kind of imagination."

I say, "Yes, you do." Have you ever pictured all the bad things that could happen to you if something went wrong? *That's* imagination. If you can do that, you have the imagination to think of all the good things that can happen when things go right.

Before we go any further, do this exercise for your legs:

··

FLIRT EXERCISE #7

Here's my card.

··

If you don't already have cards, walk to the nearest printing shop and get some made for yourself. Many print shops have a special; 1,000 in 48 hours for $20, or you can spend more and have something more fancy, humorous or business-like designed by an artist. If you want to be "socially correct," refer to an etiquette book (Emily Post, Amy Vanderbilt, Letitia Baldrige, *Vogue*, etc.) for pointers. Cards are ideal if you are tongue-tied, hurried or simply "not in the mood" to flirt. If you have already traded winks or smiles with someone, scribbling a note on the card, "Too busy to talk. Can we have coffee?" and giving it to them, tips your hand and invites them to respond. If they don't call within 48 hours—they may be busy, out of town, involved in another relationship or simply not want to call—that's fine. There are other fish in the sea, and you have the satisfaction of knowing you acted on your impulse (see chapter 4).

Cards are also great in other business and social situations. Write your request on the card and give it to the person you want to respond. Get the person's name and affiliation, and if they don't call you, you call them. They will know what you want from the card.

Cards needn't be serious. One nomadic woman I met had "Mary Smith, Waif," on hers, with no address or phone. The card of a musician friend of mine says "Michael Jones, Since 1961" (his birthdate), with address and phone. Another fellow's says, "Bob Green, At Large." In some places, the more important a person is, the larger their card is and the less information it contains. Charles DeGaulle reportedly had a 5"x 7" card with just the word "Charles" on it.

Okay, it's time for a flight of fancy.

As you can see, we are out to enjoy ourselves flirting.

To get you out there doing it, Dr. Flirt offers you a great incentive: a guarantee that you will have fun. You can't miss.

Have you ever sat back and decided against flirting because you just didn't want to deal with the people? At the same time, however, you probably thought, "Gee, I'll bet everybody else has more fun than I do."

Well, you never have to worry about that again. Now, using the Dr. Flirt Fun Graph, you can *actually quantify* the amount of fun people are having. Better yet, you can figure out exactly how much fun *you* are having, and then do something about it if you aren't having enough. Are you intrigued?

People usually describe fun on a scale from "1" to "10," as in, "How was the beach?" "It was a 10!" I therefore use that as my point value guide.

But I add another dimension: combining the Barrel of Monkeys and Fun scales. If you have more fun than a barrel of monkeys, you've got to be enjoying yourself at a level up around 10. How much fun is a barrel of monkeys? Less than 10, and more than 5. Below 5, you approach a barrel with fewer and fewer primates, until by 1 on the graph, you're left with a pretty lonely monkey. So, the Fun Graph ranges from that point, no fun, or the least fun you can have, to as much fun as a barrel of monkeys (5 or 6), to more fun than a barrel (up to 10).

Go ahead! Compute how much fun you and everybody else are having. You may find there are times when you have more fun than everybody else.

And this makes a great opening line: "Are you having more fun than me?" I don't know. Let's check the graph and see...

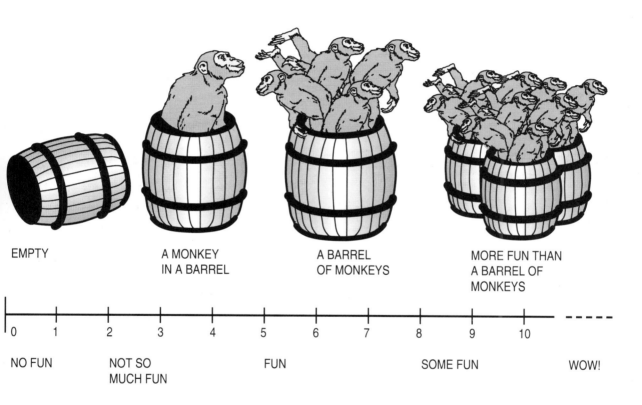

EMPTY

A MONKEY
IN A BARREL

A BARREL
OF MONKEYS

MORE FUN THAN
A BARREL OF
MONKEYS

0   1   2   3   4   5   6   7   8   9   10

NO FUN

NOT SO
MUCH FUN

FUN

SOME FUN

WOW!

3
·····

THE COMPLETE HISTORY OF FLIRTING (ABRIDGED)

This nation had a Founding Flirt.

Yes, the discoverer of lightening and weather movements, writer of *Poor Richard's Almanac*, Ambassador to France, a man who needs no introduction: Mr. Benjamin Franklin.

The portly Franklin was a gallant fellow who played double-entendre chess with the ladies of the French court, scribbled amorous notes to them and imagined consorting with them in heaven. The two things that set him apart from most 18th century men were: 1) he believed that educated women were his equals, and 2) he made friends with women as easily as men.

You may have heard of Franklin's Italian contemporary, Giovanni Casanova, who is considered a legend with women, but succeeded by using the same principles as Franklin. According to his exciting *Memoirs,* he made his fortunes and traveled the world treating men and women alike as his equals.

Franklin, Jefferson and others put this principle on paper in the Declaration of Independence and the U.S. Constitution. But that's another story.

Today, we would expect everybody to be as enlightened as Casanova and Old Ben. But slavery wasn't abolished in Europe and the United States until the mid-1800s, and women didn't get the vote until the 1920s. Many places in the world still haven't accomplished these things today.

So if you find men and women confused about relating to each other as equals here, remember that we have only been at it for about a century.

INTO THE TIME MACHINE

Before that, back to the dawn of human history (about 2,500 centuries ago), this has been a man's world. In most cultures up to this century, with rare exceptions, men's meetings with and marriages to women were arranged. Men's and women's roles were strictly defined: Women tended the home fires. Men hunted game and went to war.

The two sexes could flirt with each other, but only on the sly, because they were usually under the watchful eyes of chaperones or elders. Women were either entirely hidden, or screened by veils, clothing or accessories such as fans. Men and women flirted with their eyes and passed notes. Women were obliged to blush or swoon at compliments, men accepted them stiffly.

Thus, through the ages, *more than half* the cheering and compliments associated with flirting probably *occurred between men*. Another large portion of the winks and banter passed between the men and their concubines, courtesans, mistresses and other female acquaintances. The remaining portion passed between women, women and children and children and the elderly.

Married couples rarely flirted. It was not believed love could exist between husband and wife. Marriage was a necessary evil. Women were assumed (by men) to be inferior, and wives were held in low esteem. So, you can imagine why, with human history heavy on love and passion, the rebellious lovers' stories of Abelard and Heloise, Romeo and Juliet, Amijima and *West Side Story* are so popular.

The father of all flirting, certainly the stuff we know in our literature, was probably the Greek philosopher Plato. In the fourth century B.C., he invented a "pure" form of love, spiritual and unburdened by base carnal instincts, which made women sexless objects of male adoration. Today, of course, females and males both engage in "Platonic" love affairs, particularly high school and college students who are just discovering philosophy.

In 11th century Spain, Moorish poets added another twist to intra-sexual spirituality by inventing "courtly love." Here suitors, minstrels, troubadours, flatterers and lovesick poets stood women squarely on untouchable pedestals where they could pine for them endlessly. They introduced it to the French court at Paris, and, as you know, it spread like wildfire throughout Christendom, and even continues today as part of the chivalry western men extend toward "the weaker sex."

Other interesting notes: in Europe and America from the late 1700s on, associations and clubs of artists, literati and others came to regularly flirt, talk and make spirited repartée in the cultural centers of the day—Paris,

Berlin, Vienna, New York. Some places they just gathered for afternoon tea, some for evening soirées at salons and cafés.

Well known to Americans are those soirées of Gertrude Stein and Alice B. Toklas (of magic brownie fame) in 1920s Paris, which attracted such greats as Fitzgerald, Hemingway and Anais Nin; and in 1930s New York, the weekly Algonquin Hotel lunches of Alexander Wolcott and the likes of Dorothy Parker, Robert Benchley and the Marx brothers.

Also, former Supremes singer Mary Wilson, in her book *Dream Girls* (St. Martin's Press), describes similar flirtatious scenes around Motown Records in Detroit, when founder Barry Gordy first brought blues and gospel artists together to create "the Motown Sound." Everyone of every race loves to gather where music is played.

FLIRT STATISTICS 102
PIE CHART OF FLIRTING SINCE THE DAWN OF TIME

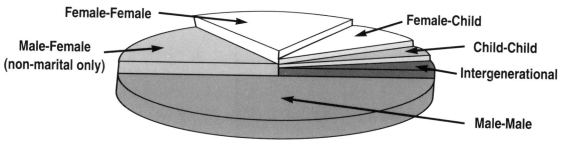

Overall, Dr. Flirt enjoys flirting best when both parties have some independence of action, when a flir*tee* and a flir*ter* can swap roles as things proceed. However, through most of history, and in many parts of the world today, the safest way to flirt is with a passing wink or raised eyebrow, a quick compliment, and that's it.

It depends on the culture. We'll cover this in more detail later, but I note here that before you flirt, you should know where and with whom who you are flirting, whether you are traveling outside your country, or meeting people right here at home. You must be sure that the flirting you do means the same thing to you as it does to the person with whom you're flirting.

If you don't get the return flirt cues from your flirtee, drop it. There are other fish in the sea.

That's flirting history in a nutshell, friends. Now, without further ado, may I present, from the beginning of time...

THE (RELATIVELY) COMPLETE LIST
OF THE WORLD'S GREATEST FLIRTS

Adam and Eve (pre-Apple)

Delilah ("Samson! What gorgeous hair!")

David and Bathsheba ("Wow!")

King Solomon ("Vanity, vanity, all is vanity.")

Cleopatra ("Would you like some tips on makeup?")

Helen of Troy ("May I help launch your ship?")

Merlin ("I'm getting younger all the time!")

Sheherazade (*Stories for 1001 Arabian Nights*)

Nostradamus ("I tell fortunes...")

The Medicis ("We know a lot of good people...")

Leonardo DaVinci ("Want to see my etchings?")

Christopher Columbus ("The world is round!")

Louis the XIV ("Don't you *love* this furniture?")

Marie Antoinette ("Let them eat cake!")

William Shakespeare ("A rose by any other name...")

Cassanova ("Ahh, *ma petite chou* (my little cabbage)")

Lady Godiva ("It's not what you say, but what you do!")

Benjamin Franklin (as noted)

George Washington ("Want to help me build a country?")

George Washington Carver ("Here, have some peanuts.")

Mata Hari ("Tell me your secrets.")

Charro ("Whee!")

Cary Grant ("Everybody wants to be Cary Grant.")

George Burns ("Pretty good for an old man, eh?")

_____ (Add your own favorite here)

GREAT MOMENTS IN FLIRTING

Another great way to understand flirting is to watch the experts do it—on stage, screen, radio and in print (comics, newspapers, books and magazines).

Anything that features interactions between two people will usually include a flirting scene somewhere.

Take Lauren Bacall and Humphrey Bogart's first movie together, *To Have and Have Not*. These two tough cookies size each other up in Steve's (Bogart's) upstairs office. They flirt outrageously with eyes and gestures, then Slim (Bacall) heads for the door, and pauses:

> *"If you want me, all you have to do is whistle. You know how to whistle, don't you, Steve? You just put your lips together, and blow."*

In *The Thin Man* detective movie series (available on video), Nick and Nora Charles are so lively and witty with each other, people have told me they wish their own marriages could be like that. Then, there are always the movies in which you expect flirtations: Southern ladies fluttering their fans in *Showboat* and *Gone with the Wind*, male-female play in *Fletch*, *Bull Durham* and *An Officer and a Gentleman*.

There are too many flirting examples on television to count, now. The longest-running male-female one is the NBC comedy "Cheers," where the bartender, Sam Malone, spends season after season wooing the barmaid, Diane Chambers, and the bar manager, Rebecca Howe. For flirting between generations, check out "Little House on the Prairie," "The Waltons," "The Wonder Years," "Northern Exposure" and "Brooklyn Bridge."

Then, catch the radio and television commercials. Foster Grant®, Coke®, Pepsi®, Maypo® cereal, Maxwell House® coffee, Molson's Beer®, Rainier Beer®, Timken Bearings®, United Airlines and U.S. Bank are just a few of the companies whose ads come to mind.

Look in places you don't expect, too. In "buddy" movies such as *Butch Cassidy and the Sundance Kid*, *The Princess Bride*, *Lethal Weapon* and *Thelma and Louise*, the main characters regularly flirt and humorously tease one another.

And look further afield. In *The Untouchables*, there are touching moments between Elliot Ness and his daughter. When he tucks her into bed she demands, "Butterflies and eskimos, Daddy." They wink their eyelashes on each other's cheeks and rub noses.

All these examples come from the theater, where men and women, friends and adversaries, young and old have been flirting since the Greek farces of Aristophenes 2,300 years ago. In Shakespeare's 17th century *Midsummer Night's Dream*, the fairy queen Titania flirts with Bottom. Modern U.S. theater always uses it. One of my favorites is the recent *Ronnie Bwana, Jungle Guide*. This send-up of 1930s white hunter movies relies on a flirting twist. Here, the white hunter is a woman, Veronica Bwana, and *she* falls in love with the professor's daughter.

Read about it, too. Flirting dates from the ancient Sirens irresistibly calling Greek sailors to abandon their ships. The first surviving work of Platonic love was written a few centuries later, by the Roman poet Ovid about the year 0: *Ars Amatoria*. More earthy stuff appears later in *The Decameron* and *Canterbury Tales*, more courtly stuff in the Lancelot legend and Chaucer's *Troilus and Cressida*. There's plenty of refined repartee in Jane Austen's *Pride and Prejudice*, and in E.M. Forster's turn-of-the-century book, *A Room with a View*.

For flirtatious songs, however, you'll have to go back a couple decades to a point before sex, love affairs and divorce became the staple subjects for lyrics. There are exceptions, such as, "My eyes adored you, though I never laid a hand on you."

Otherwise, we must go back further, (not including R&B or the Blues), to such titles as "Jeepers, Creepers" (Where'd You Get Those Peepers?), "A Pretty Girl Is Like a Melody," "Ain't We Got Fun" and "Five Foot Two, Eyes of Blue."

WHAT ABOUT REAL LIFE?

Okay, enough mental stuff.

From the annals of Dr. Flirt, let me paint a picture of a warm fall afternoon when I'd healed enough from a car accident to finally limp outside without crutches.

I just wanted to sit in an outdoor café and watch people walking by. But the deck at my favorite place was packed, and only one chair was open at a table occupied by a petite and striking woman. I asked the young restaurant hostess to introduce me, but she snapped her gum and retorted, "Why 'n' cha ask her yerself?"

So I limped over and extended my hand. "I'm harmless," I said. "I just got off crutches and want to watch people walk on two legs."

"I used to train race horses," the woman said, taking my hand in a vise-like grip. "One smashed me in the gate, so I was on crutches for a while, too. Have a seat."

"Where did you get that grip?" I asked.

"Polo," she replied.

"How does one get into polo?"

"One decides it's the most exciting game on earth, and one plays it."

As you might imagine, this meeting led to an afternoon of spirited conversation and people-watching.

Get out there and do it, friends. The air is filled with flirting.

4

•••••

GETTING DOWN TO FLIRTING

Now that I've told you to get out there and flirt, what are you gonna do? Well, you know from chapter 1 that *flirting is pressure-free*. Or it should be. But there's a big difference between talking about something and doing it. So, I'll open this chapter with another key rule:

....

THE FOURTH RULE OF FLIRTING
Take everything one step at a time.
....

See, a lot of people think that there's just one short step from a flirtatious glance to conjugal relations. They probably get that from reading too many potboiler novels, and watching too many misleading movies and television shows.

And I can see that creating a lot of terror in people. Who wants to flirt if they're afraid they'll be expected to jump into bed? Who wants to flirt when a harmless wink may antagonize someone with a bad impression?

Let's take things one step at a time. Here's another question people often ask me:

Q: If a woman/man flirts with me, does that mean she/he is interested?

A: Not necessarily. This person may just be no-contact flirting. They may also want to have a conversation, go out for coffee, or for dinner or a night on the town.

If they flirt at you, flirt back and see if they reply. If you flirt at them, see if they flirt back. If you're not sure, go ask. But don't put yourself into a pressure cooker and sit there to stew: Are they *interested* in me? How do I *look*? What do I *say*? What do we do next?

Most of us carry this amazing fantasy that people under pressure must be witty. You've watched James Bond snort bad puns as bullets whiz by his ears. You've watched Mae West keep mobs of hungry men at bay with smart one-liners. Everything we see, hear and read is packed with these daredevils who always have something nifty to say, who can take every situation in hand.

You know what makes all those daredevils so smooth?

They are totally synthetic.

They're all created by writers and artists who slave for hours or months over story boards and manuscripts, coming up with the best possible stuff for those characters to say and do.

Nobody in real life has writers.

We all wish we did. We all wish that, just once, *we* could be that smooth. We, and billions of other wishing people have created a worldwide market for this kind of fantasy.

We have even seen real-live people be fast and smooth: Winston Churchill, Bill Cosby, Dorothy Parker, Robin Williams, Joan Rivers, Johnny Carson and Arsenio Hall.

But you know what? *All of us are that smooth.* We can't spend years admiring great and innovative people without a little of them rubbing off on us.

It's just that *we* usually come up with that great line or action *after* the event, back in the privacy of our own homes where we can think about it. The Churchills, Cosbys, Parkers, Rivers and Carsons are those rare people who can think of great lines on the spot, under pressure. Remember the last time you did a zinger on the spot? You probably told people, "I can't believe I said that!" (But you *did* say it! Refer back to Flirt Exercise #5, and practice patting youself on the back and/or accepting a compliment.)

So I want a show of hands now: how many of you *enjoy* operating under pressure?

I don't see many hands. Let me illustrate what it feels like to operate under pressure.

FLIRT EXERCISE #7
Put yourself in a pressure cooker.

1. Get a piece of typing or construction paper.

2. Roll it into a cone.

3. Now look through the big end.

This is how the world looks to people under pressure: all your attention focused on a tiny space.

Imagine a football quarterback. This is what he sees after he gets the ball. He is wearing a helmet with a face guard and trying to see over a seething mass of oak tree-sized men. He has three seconds to do something with the ball before 600-pounds worth of linemen crush him to the ground.

Imagine yourself entering a room or bar full of strangers. You (anxiously) find yourself squeezing down your focus to locate the one safe haven (chair, barstool, food table) where you can feel secure enough to reconnoiter.

Now turn the cone around. Look through the small end.

This is closer to how the world really looks, even though you may not think so at the moment. It is probably how it looks to someone like the quarterback, who is accustomed to working under pressure, before he gets the ball.

Now, unfold the paper.

This is how the world really looks. The mind is an amazing thing, isn't it? Under pressure, it focuses right down to concentrate on getting through the task or event at hand. When it's relaxed, it lets you see everything. Even if you can't see everything under pressure, you don't become invisible. Think of the ostriches. Under pressure they just stick their heads in the ground for the whole world to see.

This exercise illustrates the Second Rule of Flirting: flirt where you're comfortable, flirt who you are. If you're some place where you feel pressured, you'll rarely feel comfortable, or be in the right frame of mind to flirt.

Everybody gets "butterflies." If you think yours are more serious, you may want to check under "P" or "T" in the Yellow Pages (see chapter 2), and make an appointment for some advice.

Otherwise, you will feel comfortable flirting if you take it one step at a time.

So, let's take the steps to find your own Personal Comfort Zone. The first is to define your territory. Where are you most yourself?

··

FLIRTING CHECKLIST #1
My Most Comfortable Places to Flirt

1—YES, 2—NO, 3—I COULD TRY THAT

☐ Work	☐ School	☐ Crowd
☐ Lunchroom	☐ Gallery	☐ Party
☐ Elevator	☐ Museum	☐ Bar
☐ Deli counter	☐ Ballpark	☐ Music Club
☐ Supermarket	☐ Outdoor activity	☐ Cruise Ship
☐ Bookstore	☐ Health Club	☐ Dinner
☐ Religious center	☐ Concert hall	☐ Park
☐ Library	☐ Dance clubs	☐ Telephone
☐ Cafe/Restaurant	☐ Ferry/Bus	☐ Airplane
☐ Waiting in line	☐ Wedding/Funeral	☐ Home
☐ Sports events	☐ Breakfast	☐ _____ (Other)

So, you know where you can be yourself. But you flirt *with* people. What kinds of people let you be yourself? What people share your interests?

FLIRTING CHECKLIST #2

People I'm Most Comfortable Flirting With

1—YES, 2—NO, 3—I COULD TRY THAT

- ☐ Men
- ☐ Women
- ☐ Smokers
- ☐ Non-smokers
- ☐ Studious types
- ☐ Fellow workers
- ☐ Professionals
- ☐ Tradespeople
- ☐ Secretaries
- ☐ Religious people
- ☐ Family
- ☐ Teachers
- ☐ Garage salers

- ☐ Artists
- ☐ Lawyers/politicians
- ☐ Entrepreneurs
- ☐ Outdoorsfolk
- ☐ Beer drinkers
- ☐ Espresso drinkers
- ☐ Wine drinkers
- ☐ Tea/coffee drinkers
- ☐ Musicians/singers
- ☐ Gardeners
- ☐ Friends
- ☐ The Horsey Set
- ☐ Sailors

- ☐ Engineers
- ☐ Jocks
- ☐ Students
- ☐ Travelers
- ☐ Young folk
- ☐ Mid-folk
- ☐ Old folk
- ☐ Writers
- ☐ Actors
- ☐ Managers
- ☐ Barflies
- ☐ Gays/Lesbians
- ☐ Straights

So, you have a mental picture of where your Personal Comfort Zone is, and who's in it.

Now, what are you looking for in a flirt partner? You might be surprised: everybody is looking for the same things as you! This is what people in my classes said when I asked them:

FLIRTING CHECKLIST #3
What Everyone Is Looking For

WOMEN	MEN
■ Sparkle in the eyes	■ Eyes that say 'someone's home'
■ Not so much well-dressed as well-kept	■ Neat appearance, not sloppy, well-kept
■ Hair any length, but trimmed	■ Natural look
■ Somebody who listens when I talk	■ A good listener
■ Intelligent	■ Somebody who can think
■ Sensitive, not lecturing	■ Compassionate, not mothering
■ Holds himself well	■ Projects confidence
■ Doesn't have to be handsome	■ Doesn't have to be beautiful
■ In good shape	■ In good shape

Single men and women seeking a prospective date also looked for a wedding ring as a sign of whether the prospect was available. However, they agreed as long as they kept it platonic, it was okay to flirt with married people too.

Of course, researchers have studied this (more studies in chapter 6). Both males and females want various personal qualities in their partners, but initially males place more emphasis on physical characteristics than females.

Also, a self-image study at Michigan State University found that males who were thin or overweight, and females who were overweight, both felt stigmatized in society. Your best bet if you feel this way is to cultivate skills, hobbies, collections or activities of your own which make you feel good about yourself (see Exercise #4). These personal enrichment pursuits can also put you together with people of similar interests (Flirt Rule #2) and open doors for you to more contacts with people you want to meet.

The good thing about flirting is that it is harmless and asexual, which makes it an ideal way for anyone of any size or sex to interact with people, and let the good spirits inside them show through.

And that's the point of finding your Personal Comfort Zone. Wherever you go, you'll be able to find people who have a lot in common with you, and with whom you'll feel comfortable to flirt or strike up a conversation.

You like to speak? Join Toastmasters or a speaker's bureau. You don't like bars or singles clubs? Don't go to them. You like the outdoors? Try Volksmarch, mountaineering, bicycling or skiing clubs. You want to meet wealthy people? Try yachting, polo, antique cars, flower and animal shows and country clubs. You like business? Try sales and training outfits, lodges (Lions, Elks, Eagles, Shriners, Rotary, etc.), the City Club, chambers of commerce. Charity work? Try Jaycees, service clubs, soup kitchens and volunteer outfits.

Between your telephone book and your local newspapers, you'll find interest groups for everything from computers to crocheting, horseshoes to HAM radio.

Time to warm up for flirting. Got your courage up? Try this over the next day or week—however you feel comfortable:

··

FLIRT EXERCISE #8
Practice the flirt-a-day method.

··

Day 1: Play peek-a-boo with a baby or child.

Day 2: Compliment yourself about something in the mirror.

Day 3: Compliment a family member.

Day 4: Compliment a co-worker, or someone at school.

Day 5: Smile at somebody you don't know.

Day 6: Ask a question of a complete stranger.

Day 7: Rest.

5
• • • • •

DEALING WITH SUCCESS AND REJECTION

You've established your Personal Comfort Zone, so you're ready to flirt. You go out, you flirt with somebody and you realize you have piqued their interest. Inadvertently, you have backed into an important choice. Do you want to meet this person or not? If not, just go about your business. If so, then practice:

....

THE FIFTH RULE OF FLIRTING

Approach your prospect immediately.

Do not wait.

....

Do not agonize. Do not give yourself time to break into a cold sweat. Just walk over and ask. Pick up the telephone and call. Send the note.

Are you sweating now? (I won't mince words here. Whether you're a man or a woman, you *sweat* in a tight situation). "You mean, now, Dr. Flirt? Wait, wait! I've gotta think about this!"

You may fear this moment of action, the moment you'll either get the "Yes" or "No." You are making your life hinge on an instant, where you give somebody else the power to tell you whether you are okay to keep them company.

No wonder you shy away!

The moment you make eye contact with that person, or get them on the phone, you can almost feel the meter start running. Am I right? In a flash, you are in contact. The Greeks had a concept for this: Mercury, Messenger of the Gods. He flew "fast as thought" to do the gods' bidding.

Well, calm yourself, friends. You already know you're acceptable (Flirt Exercises #2, #3 and #5). You're looking and feeling the best you possibly can. You *know* what the other person is looking for (Flirt Checklist #3).

Take a deep breath. Repeat Exercise #7 to put this pressure in perspective. And read on.

Both you *and* your prospect know the meter is running. You *both* know this is a flirting game. You *both* know that you'll either connect, so you can pursue this contact and flirt some more, or you won't, and you'll move on. It's that simple. (Even if you don't connect this time, you may get a second chance! This person may not feel like flirting now, but may want to later. Suggest that option to them).

For those of you with butterflies, try the following:

···

FLIRT EXERCISE #9

Three, two, one!
···

1. Select the person you want to flirt with.

2. Go flirt with two *other* people first.

3. Now that you've practiced, flirt with your first selection.

The longer you wait to call or approach your person, the bigger they get. Honest.

Your mind comes up with all the reasons you shouldn't do this, why this won't work, why this person will say no, how you'll save face, etc. etc. etc. And what you succeed in doing is building a mountain between yourselves.

And friends, it gets higher with every reason you invent.

When you finally *do* make the approach, you have to scale that mountain to get to your person. So you drag yourself to the top, where you have put that person yourself, and you manage to squeak out your compliment or request in the thin air up there. Suppose that person says no? You've got a long way to fall!

Don't wait. Go for it.

Again, use your imagination to think of all the reasons this works for you.

SPACE: THE FINAL FRONTIER
—*Star Trek*

There's one more important issue: space.

Whenever you approach someone for the first time, be mindful that you can only get "so" close.

If you telephone, for example, there are certain acceptable times to call—before 10 P.M. every night, and on weekends, after 9:30 A.M. Show some respect. Let the poor dears sleep.

Each of us has a personal area around us. We feel comfortable in this space, and strangers must respect it or risk rejection or repulsion. This is a key to making first contact, and to avoiding that sticky situation called "harassment" (see chapter 6). You may breach another person's boundary thinking it'll get their attention, and it does, but it may also get you the attention of big friends, bouncers, police, lawyers, men and women's groups and the American public.

This is important, folks, particularly for men. We are just seeing the tip of the iceberg on man/woman personal space violations. As I noted in chapter 3, we've spent most of recorded history locked into specific "pursuing male-docile female" roles, and the transition to equal partnership is bound to be a rocky road since we're doing it for the first time this century.

Most women have been taught to not be confrontational. So if they don't want your attention, they may remain silent, try to graciously change the subject or to excuse themselves. Many males may have been told this is some form of come-on, or that if you can make a woman uncomfortable, she'll respect you.

Not true. She is seriously *not interested*. Back off.

When you see a man or woman sitting alone in a room, café or bar, don't sit down in the seat next to them. Sit one seat away. They know you're approaching. They know the game. It's no secret. Give them space. After you've got the initial go-ahead, you may be allowed inside that space.

I was on a radio show one afternoon, and a young man called in to say the best way to flirt with a woman was to take hold of her wrist, look deeply into her eyes, and say, seriously, "You're the one. I've been looking for you all my life."

Bad idea. So bad, it could be dangerous to your health.

This violates the woman's space, and her sense of propriety. The best you can expect from this "grab" technique is rejection. The worst is physical harm from whomever she calls to her rescue.

START THE CHASE

So let's take a step back and examine how to finesse that new acquaintanceship without the physical contact. This is the ideal point to come full circle, back to my first point in this chapter, which is: You are ready to flirt.

Sometimes, it seems as if everything in life happens when you are least ready for it, and you least expect it. Yet you make it through, don't you? You make the best of the situation, and you're probably surprised you have done as well as you did.

M. Scott Peck, in his book *The Road Less Traveled*, asserts that everybody leads a charmed life. Basically, if you have managed to survive up to this point, avoiding car crashes, diseases, occupational accidents, acts of God and whatever, you are "charmed." That puts a new spin on meeting someone. You shake their hand and say, "Charmed, I'm sure." Try it as an opening line, too: "Hey, I hear you lead a charmed life."

Huey Lewis, the rock and roll star, got his first Grammy after he had spent almost 20 years singing and playing in rock bands. In his acceptance speech, he said, "Thanks for making me an overnight sensation."

When Mr. Lewis got the Grammy, he didn't come out of nowhere. He was ready for it.

That is what this book is about. I don't teach swimming by heaving somebody into a pool, sink or swim. I believe people become successful by believing in their own charmed lives, and preparing for the opportunities that come along.

Who knows, you may be holding this book in a café, minding your own business, when somebody stops and says, "A book on flirting? Gee, I coulda written one twice that size!"

And that's the whole point here. You've found your Personal Comfort Zone. Now, to play the game of flirting, you want to pique the interest of your flirtee, so they flirt back, call back, write back, approach you or otherwise invite you to flirt some more.

THE SIXTH RULE OF FLIRTING
When you flirt, create movement— a gentle chase.

See, the original "chase" dates from the dawn of history. If you regard the animals as our ancestors, you can see that we come by pursuit naturally. All sorts of species playfully chase each other at any opportunity they get. Watch puppies and dogs, kittens and cats, otters, horses and dolphins whenever you have the chance.

But here's a warning: As you watch the animals, don't confuse the spring mating action for play. It's not. When the males chase the females, that is serious hunting. And so is all that bellowing and squawking, displaying plumage and butting heads that accompanies it. Early in human history, our homo sapiens forbears chased mates in similar fashion. For example, just watch movies like *Tarzan*, *King Kong*, *Quest for Fire* or *Clan of the Cave Bear*.

If you watch children, they constantly chase each other. In fact, that's the basis for half of their games: tag, hide-and-seek, capture the flag, soccer, rugby, football, baseball. Come to think of it, adults play this way, too.

As we evolved through history, several factors contributed to refining the human chase process. We developed nuances of language, we moved indoors to better digs, we improved our dress, invented props (parasols, fans, veils, twistable mustaches, ties, hats, sunglasses), learned about our emotional sides, and developed complex social patterns for relating to one another.

Today, if you're an adult who wants to flirt, you don't simply pull someone's hair and dash away, or swat them and yell, "Tag! You're it!" No, if you're an adult (or you're pretending to be adult), your flirting must be more polished.

Two "more polished" flirting techniques come to mind, because they have evolved with our changing fashions for centuries: (1) The lady dropping her daintily embroidered handkerchief near the gentleman who interests her, in hopes he would retrieve it, chase after her and ask politely, "Did you drop this?" and (2) the man shaking his pack of cigarettes toward a man or woman to break the ice: "Smoke?"

Though handkerchieves have lost their popularity, and cigarettes are on the way out, both these gestures are still employed. The handkerchief ploy is now done with papers and other personal items, dropped in front of the prospect, or left conspicuously, but "accidentally," for the intended person to retrieve. The "smokes" ploy is a play on the age-old invitation to "break bread" and share food with friends.

You can create a chase by conspicuously picking up the wrong item from a table or cloakroom—a briefcase, umbrella or bag, and catching the attention of its owner before you walk away with it. Hopefully, you and the owner will have traded some glances beforehand, and the owner will chase you down, rather than call the police.

Foster Grant, in fact, made a television commercial along this line several years ago. A woman asks a handsome man if she can try on his sunglasses. He says yes, she tries them on, then puts them in her purse. When he expresses surprise, she simply hands him her card, and tells him the name of the hotel where he can find her.

Both these "capture-the-flag" capers—the cloakroom and sunglasses snatches—border on hunting, however. I don't recommend them unless both you and your prospect have advanced to a level of the game where you intend to make a date anyway.

The cigarette ploy is still around, too, but today, packets of gum or snacks, a cup at the punchbowl, even a handful of snatched wildflowers, have generally replaced the pack of smokes as the means to attract a prospect in your direction.

So, that's how to set up the chase when you are in the mood to make contact. Catch the interest of the man or woman, and entice him or her to play the game of flirting with you.

Now, a flirting scenario may happen by accident, as you unintentionally create interest, and get approached. For example, you may wave or speak in a crowded area, or call a name that many people in the room turn out to have. Then, someone in the line of sight, or close earshot, responds, "Were you calling me?" or "Did you mean me?" If that happens, you have two choices: decline, or go with it. If you have the leisure to get sidetracked, you might enjoy having a bit of conversation, trading cards or inviting the surprise person out for a cup of java or tea. Or maybe you can laugh about the mistake, have a moment of fun and part ways.

Again, what you are doing by this flirting give-and-take, is creating a gentle chase. And remember, we have been chasing each other since we were children, since the time we achieved self-awareness, around the age of five. What you are doing is just a refinement of a game you already know quite well.

Now, maybe you don't feel you're ready to actually interact with someone. Maybe you're afraid of being burned.

That's where we get concerned about what to do when the person *you're interested in* turns out to be *interested in you.*

I was watching women with a buddy of mine awhile back, and suddenly he turned to me and demanded, "You know what's wrong with all these women? After you meet them, they all become people!"

Women could say the same of men.

That's why no-contact flirting is so appealing. You never have to worry if you're just doing it in the mirror.

Deciding to meet someone adds a whole new dimension to the flirting process. And it makes many people uncomfortable. We are afraid that when these folks we've been watching "become people," they'll reject us. I'm not just writing to singles here. Everyone has this fear.

So, let's take a step backward.

Before you take any action in your Personal Comfort Zone, you must learn to read.

Imagine you are taking a walk in the forest. Suddenly, you see a deer. You grab your camera and shoot a nature picture. You get the film developed, and there in your beautiful picture of the deer is a garbage can and an outhouse. You don't remember seeing those!

··

THE SEVENTH RULE OF FLIRTING
"Read" the person and situation where
you want to flirt.

··

Professional photographers "frame" the photo before they shoot. That is, they look at the whole scene through the camera lens first, so they avoid including items that won't work in the finished picture.

It's exactly the same in flirting. You look at the whole scene before heading in to flirt. Reading the person and the situation now saves you embarrassment in many forms later.

This comes straight out of Flirting Exercise #7, The Pressure Cooker. Pretend you're looking through the small end of the cone. Or that you're looking at the scene without any cone at all.

Let's start with the big picture. Several people I know reach for the Yellow Pages® the moment they arrive in a new town or city. The different listings there answer all sorts of questions for them. Does the mix of businesses reveal a white-collar town (heavy on attorneys, drycleaners, engineers, newspapers and magazines, physicians and therapists), a blue collar town (heavy on construction, design-engineering, manufacturing, tools, transportation and related services), or is it mixed? What industries sustain the town? Is it a trading center, a port, a headquarters town? What does it value? Sports teams, symphony, theater, trade schools, colleges? Are the people predominantly older or younger? Can you tell the racial mix? Lots of bookstores, restaurants? Do the pizza and fast food places dominate? Or does the mix include diners and fine eateries, too?

Many travelers and nomads I know even go a step further. During their first days in the new place, they seek out the shops and services they'll depend on to give them a sense of comfort—a good greeting card store, a comfy café or neighborhood bar, the right supermarket, the library, a good jogging or bicycling route. By shopping at several places in a day for an item or two at a time, they learn the lay of the land, take in the air, see the people and get good exercise, too.

And they meet people along the way, just by asking questions about their new surroundings. One of the most appealing approaches is inviting assistance from those around you. Appeal is the very essence of flirting. People love to help other people, and that works in your favor, whether you are new in a town or not.

The key to your comfort and success in any new situation is being prepared.

Q: Wait a minute, Dr. Flirt. This is a cold-blooded approach. I mean, isn't flirting supposed to be spontaneous?

A: Of course it is. In flirting, you want to be spontaneously *outgoing*, not spontaneously retreating. You achieve that when you feel self-confident in the situation. And the best way to do that is to first examine and understand the situation in which you are about to place yourself. Then you can decide whether you want to be there at all. You have that choice, you know.

Years ago, I ran into a therapist who showed me an exercise. He held up two hands and asked me, "Do you want chocolate, or vanilla?"

"Chocolate," I replied. I love chocolate.

Then he asked me, "Do you want chocolate or vanilla?"

"I just told you. I want chocolate."

"Do you want chocolate or vanilla?" he repeated.

Now, I was getting annoyed. "I don't get this," I said.

"Do you want chocolate or vanilla?"

"Forget it. I don't want to play this game."

"Good answer," he complimented me.

Remember, you always have the option of *not* choosing any available alternative, just as you have the option of choosing one. It all depends on whether or not you see just what you want.

LEARNING TO READ

We rarely read a scene with people closely. We've been taught it's impolite to stare. Fine. Don't stare. Take a few *polite* close looks. How else will you get a sense of who he or she is, and whether you want to approach him or her?

If you want to find out more about reading people than you'll ever use, try Julius Fast's *Body Language* (Simon & Schuster) and *Subtext* (Viking), and Robert Whiteside's *Face Language* (Simon & Schuster).

Generally, there are several questions to ask yourself as you proceed with your "read":

THE OFFICIAL FLIRT READING LESSON

- What does this person's body language tell you? Do they look open or closed? Is your prospect out in the open or in a corner? Are the legs and arms crossed or not? How is this person postured? Sitting or standing? Upright? Relaxed? Hunched? Tense? Is this person with people or alone? Talking or listening? Animated? Impatient? Serious? Neutral?

- What does this person's face tell you? Age? Laugh lines? Are they enjoying themselves? Sad? Fatigued? Angry?

- What does this person's appearance tell you? Sloppy? Well-kept? Just off work? Fresh from the shower? In good shape?

- Who is around this person, and what do they tell you about the company this person keeps? What is this person doing?

- What does this person's clothing and/or jewelry tell you? Is it expensive or inexpensive? Obvious,understated, exotic, plain? Is there a watch? What kind (Rolex, plastic Casio or Timex Triathalon)? Which wrist (if left, they're right-handed; if right, they're left-handed).

Why do I stress this kind of observation?

So that you don't rush clumsily into a situation that will sour you on flirting. You want to enjoy this!

As you can see, this exercise is anything but cold-blooded. It satisfies the curiosity every child has about people. So, treat your inner child. And in the process, you protect your adult. Reconnoitering the situation is simple, common sense. It's the same principle as defensive driving. Nobody wants to get themselves into places where they don't want to be.

The key to flirting is making it *look* easy and light. It's the same as professional athletes making their sports look effortless. You *know* they've put in years of practice to make it look that way. And it shows.

You don't have to invest years to become a flirting "pro." But you *do* have to practice. Just as you must practice anything to become proficient. Remember: flirting is a skill you can learn. That's how *everybody* gets good at it. There are no "natural" flirts except infants, puppies and kittens.

· ·

FLIRT READING TEST

Q: Who is more approachable?

    a. A gal with spiked hair, leather, rivets, pointed boots and mirrored sunglasses?

    b. A guy wearing comfy cotton pants, sandals and a v-necked shirt?

    c. Both, neither, or a. or b.

· ·

The correct answer is **c.** The guy in the comfy cotton pants could be a dangerous drug dealer. The gal in the leather outfit could just be costumed for a night of dancing at clubs.

Of course, your own first impression is a key to answering this question. Based on *your* years of experience and observation, how do *you* read this scene? From *that*, you decide whether or not each of these people is approachable. With your vivid imagination, you can even make up a story about each one's whole life.

Who is the woman sitting in a business suit with a briefcase in a hotel lobby at 10 P.M.? An executive? A courier? Or the guy in suspenders and hip waders? Fisherman? Fireman? Stockbroker?

We are most likely to approach people who smile, whose arms are open, and who appear genuinely happy to see us. We are most likely to avoid people who give us the once-over from tables in dark corners, where they sit, smoking and hunched over a drink.

READ 'EM AND...

So, you have read the scene, satisfied yourself that it is to your liking, and you flirt with this person, using an item from the Complete List of Proven Flirting Techniques in chapter 1.

Then, your prospect follows The Fifth Rule of Flirting, and gives chase. Now, you're ready to make contact.

"But wait!" you choke. "I don't meet people well. I can never think of anything to say."

In your Personal Comfort Zone, you don't *have* to think of something fresh to say. How can you? I mean, as long as 3,000 years ago, King Solomon (a.k.a. Ecclesiastes) was singing, "There is nothing new under the sun!"

DR. FLIRT'S CONVERSATION 101
Ask about the weather.

I once had a neighbor, Mr. Watson, who sat at his row house window all day watching the neighborhood. I came out of my house one sunny, sweet-smelling spring day, and said, "Mr. Watson, I wish every day was like this."

"I don't," he growled. "What would people talk about?"

All those etiquette books I mentioned in Exercise #7 say the same thing as Mr. Watson: most conversations begin with simple topics, such as your surroundings and the weather. Then they develop into chats about furniture, house projects, sailing, travel and walking the dog.

You'd be surprised where things go.

You could even ask about star signs. Star signs are so far out now, they're back in.

That master Dale Carnegie, who wrote *How to Win Friends and Influence People*, says listening is one of the most powerful tools he ever found for conversation. In fact, the more you listen, the more intelligent people think you are.

Of course, you can't *both* be the most intelligent. Somebody's got to start the conversation, and somebody's got to reply.

Here's another pointer. Recall the maxim from journalism school: every good news story answers these questions: Who? What? When? Where? Why? and How? They're known as the "Five Ws and an H." Good coversations answer those questions, too.

DR. FLIRT'S CONVERSATION 102
Ask about, or remark upon, things you have in common.

For example, you are both in the same place (Where? Why are you there? When do things start? Who is this person? How did they get there?). Next, you are both doing the same things (What? How?). And, you are both observing the same things.

Now, I have been very positive about things up to this point. But I must admit that there are exceptions to the rules.

For example, suppose you find yourself *outside* your own Personal Comfort Zone, yet you see someone you want to flirt with. This may be at the office party, walking at the waterfront park, shopping at a store, or in a bar.

Or, suppose you start a conversation and it goes nowhere.

Or, suppose you flirt and nobody flirts back, or worse yet, rejects your advance!

Suddenly, you feel yourself starting to sweat! (Again!).

All this work! Why'd I buy this book!? What do I *do*? Am I going to be rejected?

FEAR OF REJECTION

Let's just forget the whole thing, right?

Wrong.

Remember the Fourth Rule of Flirting: Take this one step at a time.

Now, why do you think people would say, "No" to you? Here's the list. See how many items you can control:

FLIRT CHECKLIST #4
Why They Say, "No" and
What You Can Do About It

REASON	CAN YOU CONTROL IT?	METHOD
You have:		
Bad breath	Yes	Mints, gum, toothbrush
Body odor	Yes	Deodorant, cologne, shower
Rumpled appearance	Yes	Straighten out, brush up
Tied tongue	Yes	"Read" your prospect; use a card or note; try Conversation 101 and 102
Bad mood	Yes	Don't flirt; wear a mood-changing disguise or expression; find something else to do.
Your prospect:		
Does not interpret your gambit as flirting	Maybe	Explain yourself
Feels cranky or ill	No	
Was fired	No	
Was rejected already	No	
Had a tragedy	No	
Wants to be alone	No	
Doesn't respond	No	
Is waiting for someone	No	
Is married or otherwise attached to a jealous partner	No	
Has a disease	No	
Lives only for work	No	
Just doesn't like or feel comfortable with you	No	

As you can see from this list, you *can* do something about things that have to do with you. You *can't* do anything about things that have to do with other people.

Now, if you're really hung up on rejection, wear a button that says, "Tell me 'NO,' I Can Take It." That gets things out front right away. Then you can forget about it. People will ask you, "Wait a minute. Does that have something to do with "Just Say 'No' to Drugs?" And you say, "No. It has to do with, do you want to dance?"

But why wear a sign that says, "Reject me"? Take a positive approach. Being rejected will probably make you feel down. But you're a grownup, and you can take care of yourself. There are a lot of people out there, and if one says, "No," the next one will probably say, "Yes." And if not, use the advice from a spunky young dude who attended one of my seminars:

"When I get a 'No' three times in a row, I go home for the night," he says. "I just figure my biorhythms are off. There's always another night." And another day.

Now, I'll level with you. It rarely feels good to be turned down (except when some good-hearted person [parent or friend] tries to set you up on a date with somebody, and you make the call hoping that person will say no). Even Dr. Flirt is hurt by rejection.

But if you feel good about yourself, your satisfaction and joy are your strengths. If you have taken care of what you can control, you'll understand that your prospect is taking care of him- or herself when he or she says "No." Congratulate that person.

The truth is, that's the kind of person you *want* to associate with. Somebody who takes care of him- or herself. They make the best friends and partners. Perhaps it won't be this particular one. Perhaps it will, but another time. They may be so surprised you understand them, they'll give you a second chance.

You may wonder what you should do if you get a "No," after you've already crossed a room or street to reach your person.

Is there anything else to do now that you are there? Can you continue on, buy a drink, run an errand, talk with or ask someone else to dance? "Read" the new situation and decide.

New York "flirtologist" Shellie Fraddin advises that you never go to the supermarket just to flirt. Go to shop, too. That way if you don't meet anybody, at least you've got your groceries. Never just go out looking for someone. It never works. You "telegraph" a desperate feeling of need.

If you need to go out, carry a book or the paper, and leave your expectations at home. Most good things happen by accident. You could meet someone, make friends, then meet friends of theirs—and pretty soon, you're part of a great, new crowd.

LIFE IS SIMPLE UNTIL YOU ADD PEOPLE

The great thing about puppies and babies is that they give you unconditional acceptance whenever you appear. Adults are different, but after you learn the score here, you may find people much easier to handle.

And while we're on the subject, if somebody approaches you, here's how you can graciously say, "No":

DR. FLIRT'S HOW TO SAY "NO" GUIDE

No, thank you.

Thank you, I'm flattered, but I'm not interested.

Thank you, no. I'm waiting for someone (like the Messiah).

No thanks. My religion forbids me from dancing/drinking.

Thanks, but I'm not here to meet new people. I'm just here to watch.

Thank you, I'd just like to be alone.

I'm married/attached.

My husband/wife/partner wouldn't understand.

Would you like to meet my husband/wife/partner?

I'm just taking time out here to watch people a little. Thanks anyway.

I, uh, have a disease.

Thank you, I think you are a wonderful person, but I don't think you're my type.

No thanks—I was just:
   on my way to the bathroom.
   going to make a telephone call.
   on my way home.
   leaving to rescue the babysitter.
   on my way to work. I'm on swing/graveyard this week.
   leaving for another club/party/function.
   waiting for my friends/relatives, and I think I see them!

You may never have taken the opportunity to tell anyone, "No." So go ahead. Practice. Indulge your inner child. Try out a couple of "No's" now. This is a necessary skill for staying healthy. It has to do with taking care of yourself.

Q: Suppose a guy doesn't want to take "No" for an answer?

A: First, use one of the "No's" from the "How to Say No Guide." If that doesn't work, keep your composure. The key thing is to get out where there are witnesses. Most pesterers will back off from shame in public, or if you make a scene or attach yourself to a group. You also have friends around. In a bar or club, turn to the bartender, the bouncer, and/or the telephone, which links you to cab companies and the police. Bartenders and bouncers are adept at handling these situations. In a public place, turn to another man, or to people on the street, and simply join them, explaining your problem. They will usually help you out.

Q: What do I do if somebody with a different sexual orientation than me flirts with me?

A: As long as it's just flirting, no problem. Enjoy the cheer and repartee. But if it becomes a sexual advance, and you don't want it, be tactful and clear. Just say, "This is flattering, but I'm not interested." Then move away, if they don't first.

Another note: You may run across a person of a different sexual or philosophical persuasion who approaches you *because* they are different, and think they will be the one (or ones) who'll enable you to change yourself, or "see the light." Avoid these people. At the very least, they make bad flirting prospects because they're more interested in taking care of you than taking care of themselves. At worst, you'll end up in some ugly discussion in which they try to discount your perfectly valid views and beliefs.

Q: How can I know that the person I say "Yes" to won't expect too much?

A: This is a matter of defining things clearly between yourselves from the beginning. Anyone who asks you to dance, date or drink is making a proposition to you, and your agreement creates a verbal contract. You wouldn't sign a written contract without reading it first. Likewise, don't agree to any social contract without establishing the details. It is easier to settle on the details beforehand than to waste time and energy with excuses, regrets and complaints afterward.

I posed a couple questions earlier in the chapter about what to do when you find yourself outside your Personal Comfort Zone. You have some time to think about the answers. Now, take a look and see how yours compare with Dr. Flirt's:

PROBLEM:

You find yourself outside your Personal Comfort Zone.

SOLUTIONS:

- Don't flirt. Find a chair, read a book.
- Leave the area for a safer harbor.
- Read the situation (The Seventh Rule of Flirting). Maybe you can feel comfortable with people in this scene after all.
- Do the Pressure Cooker Exercise.

Let's say you decide you can be comfortable, you flirt with someone, and you try to start a conversation. Now, I assume you have "read" your prospect, and are working at the Conversation 101 or 102 level or both. But you hit a snag.

PROBLEM:

You start a conversation and it goes nowhere.

SOLUTIONS:

- Experiment with finding common ground.
- Realize that perhaps this person you chose doesn't want to talk, or you have little or nothing in common.
- Accept your discomfort. Do them and yourself a favor. You'll free each other to find more productive conversation partners.

Dr. Flirt does not advocate contract negotiations anytime someone asks you to dance. But he does advocate that you be clear on what you want, and on the intentions of your potential dance partner. If there's any question, ask. You want to make a responsible, self-informed decision. The same thing applies for dating. If you aren't sure what your suitor expects, ask. You want to both be clear on your separate intentions beforehand, so you can avoid the embarrassment of miscommunicating later.

Things may get more delicate here, because you are getting near the thin line between making good conversation and imposing yourself on your prospect. This is where I get another Most-Asked Question:

Q: Dr. Flirt, what do members of the opposite sex want? They're a complete *mystery to me!*

A: I'm not surprised at the confusion. Men and women want the same things, but in different order from each other. It's all part of learning each other's language. Fortunately, if you're reading this book, you all speak English, so you have a common starting point for communication.

GETTING PERSONAL

At this point, I must digress in order to tell my gentle single readers what you will miss when you learn to flirt: You may never be prompted to place or respond to a personal ad again.

As an accomplished flirter, you'll lose the motivation to use a newspaper for attracting or hunting your imaginary ideal person. I mean, face it: Most people fudge the truth about themselves in their ads. A "management executive for a major corporation" often turns out to be an assistant in the Woolworth housewares department. Someone who asserts that he or she is "in good shape" may not mean they are capable of strenuous exercise. Furthermore, research shows that men and women ask for different things in their ads.

When you learn to flirt, you'll be able to say goodbye to all that. You can flirt, meet and strike up conversations with all the people you want, in person, with complete honesty, whenever you please. This will save you a lot of time and money, and build your self-esteem, too.

According to a study done at Kyoto University, each human being needs a partner, and chooses that person to confirm his or her own habits, feelings and ideals. Flirting frees you to find that person at your own pace, on your own terms.

I'm not against personal ads. I cannot count the number of people I know who have placed and responded to them. The ads make amusing reading, but none of these people has developed a serious relationship with a personal ad acquaintance. Now, some people swear by these ads, and some may have successfully used them to find their soul-mates, but generally, they are counter-productive.

Why? Most of your time is probably committed already. You have a job, friends, relatives, hobbies, maybe even a pet. If you play the personals, where do you fit the time in your schedule to meet a lot of strangers with whom you may have nothing in common?

And the actual research in this area is pretty cold. Studies of research subjects, and of 800 personal ads from East and West Coast newspapers, reveal that males tend to place emphasis on the physical characteristics of the people they want to meet (the "Playboy Centerfold Syndrome"). Females emphasize the personal and psychological aspects. Generally, personal ads for homosexuals focus more narrowly on sexuality. Heterosexual ads covered a broader range of activities.

I ask you, if you don't find it one of the most enjoyable pursuits in your life, do you have the energy, time and money to go through the personal ads process anymore?

Instead, Dr. Flirt bids you read on, to learn what men and women are really like, so you can better prepare to meet them on your own.

Now, I'll translate the lanugages of men and women.

MEN!

Men have been brought up in a physical, hierarchical world. They value independence and competition, and they always want to know where they fit in the hierarchy of who's best, most skilled, smartest, toughest.

Their conversation flows out of that. They say, "Hi, how ya doin'?" but beyond that, they care less initially about how the other guy feels than about what the other guy has accomplished. They want to start with the big picture. They'll get to the details later.

So they start off talking about what they are *doing*, what equipment or problems they are working with (i.e., jobs, stereo equipment, cars), what their favorite sports teams, heroes or politicians are doing and not doing.

Personal feelings get in the way of action people. Men are action people. They don't want to be slowed down; they don't want their independence hindered.

So you'll often see them standing or sitting at angles to each other, looking around as they talk. Why? Because, as any animal you've seen, these guys are positioned to spring into action at a moment's notice. This often makes women nervous. But, men believe they are there to solve problems, rescue maidens, set things right.

Generally, after they've accomplished or completed something, on their own or as part of a team, men may comfortably talk about how they feel. And, a change is afoot. Men are talking about their feelings in general conversation more and more. This is a result of the new sensitivity that has been emerging since the '70s, and has become the current Men's Movement, wherein men can be strong even as they are vulnerable.

WOMEN!

Women have been raised in a world of communities. They value accomplishment just as much as men do, but they are taught to make it the result of mutual, cooperative efforts rather than of independent acts. They tend to be concerned that members of the community are healthy, participating, and taken care of.

Their conversations usually start with messages about how they *feel*, such as, "Your hair looks great!" We all demonstrate how we feel by how we take care of ourselves. Women closely observe these things—hair, jewelry, clothing—then move on to feelings about relationships, work, children. They know that from these details, the big picture will paint itself.

This attention to detail is supposedly why women are better at flirting than men. Don't believe it. In the competitive world of courtship rituals, men can be just as adept. And women can be clumsy about details if they have other things on their minds.

In women's conversations, they intersperse talk about projects and accomplishments, and sports and politics, with the talk about feelings and the health of the community. Women get just as much done as men. They just do it in a different way.

And that brings up a couple of conflict points between men and women.

When men complain about things, it's because they want a problem to be solved. When women complain, they trust that things will work out, and are mainly looking for reassurance from the community. So, faced with complaints in a conversation, women offer mutual problem stories, which upsets men, who push solutions to clear up the problem, which upsets women.

Because women are set up for community, when they converse, they don't stand or sit as if they're ready to dash away. They face each other, hold each other's eyes and trade details. This, of course, can make men nervous.

Even as women have emerged since the '70s as powers in the workplace, they have not taken on the male conversational style, unless they're in a group of men, where the problem-solving, objective mode tends to dominate. Otherwise, they assemble the big picture from the important details.

MEN AND WOMEN!

There are several books out now about how you can make someone fall in love with you, get them into bed or under your influence, all by following a programmed course of calculated phrases and actions. You feed them the right lines, get into their space at the right moment, and *voila*, they are yours.

I don't like these books. They just subvert innocent flirting techniques for the purpose of hunting. And that is, or borders on being dishonest—both to you and the person you plan to approach.

I remember a seminar I attended once, where halfway through, a member of the audience yelled at the speaker, "You're trying to brainwash us!"

The speaker retorted, "You came in here brainwashed!"

What does this have to do with flirting? Well, you can study conversational styles, use catchy lines and techniques to convince someone you are on his or her "wavelength." But don't do it unless you are certain this is who you are (The Second Rule of Flirting), and that you are being honest with yourself and your prospect. The techniques you use are designed to win other people's trust and respect for you. Use them for good, not for evil.

If you must be dishonest to get what you want, Dr. Flirt suggests you rethink your goals.

Having said that, let's take a moment to have some fun with these techniques. They include "mirroring" postures and behaviors, and observing the prospect closely so you can determine what "type" they are.

You can try it out right now.

· ·

FLIRT EXERCISE #10

Look up from this book. Find someone
sitting at a table. Change your posture
to mirror theirs.

· ·

You may notice that, when you are sitting and talking with someone—family member, colleague or stranger—you find yourselves assuming the same postures, for example, leaning on an arm, playing with hair or lifting your cups to drink at the same time.

Supposedly, if you consciously practice it with your prospects (or family members, fellow students or colleagues), you will understand them better and improve your relationship.

You can mirror breathing (provided they aren't wearing bulky clothing). People who relax next to one another—lovers, babies and mothers—tend to end up breathing at the same rate.

There is also a raft of techniques for mirroring conversation, and deciding whether your conversational partner is the type of person who emphasizes the visual (seeing), aural (hearing) or feeling (sensual) sides of life, or a combination of them.

Again, all that lies outside the scope of this flirting book. If you want to know more about it, check the bibliography or head for your nearest library and check out "Neuro Linguistic Processing (NLP)," "Postural Congruence" or "Confluence."

I believe the best way to develop rapport is through dynamic interaction. If you both know it's a game, these activities can be fun, instructive and turn into a good time on a CreativeDate (see chapter 7). At best, discreetly using them may help you develop rapport with your prospects, colleagues, children and/or fellow students. At worst, the person(s) to whom you are trying to apply them will find it artificial and annoying.

Now you know everything there is to know about human psychology. Go out and flirt!

6

•••••

FLIRTING ON THE JOB,
AT SCHOOL AND ON THE FLY

To start this chapter, I must kill a myth about the workplace: sexy clothing and behavior will not help you get ahead.

Work may be a good place to meet people, but the reason people go there is to get jobs done. Being sensual where you work is, at the very least, inappropriate.

There are exceptions to this rule. If you work in the "creative side" of the media (advertising, marketing, print, broadcast), in entertainment, bars, strip clubs or out of your home—sexy apparel and talk may be appropriate. But even people who work at sexy lingerie shops and adult bookstores dress conservatively.

If you're in manufacturing, finance, insurance, apparel, wholesale, retail, travel, leaning on sex just tells people you don't understand or accept: 1) your role at the workplace, 2) the way business is done, and 3) how you're expected to relate to co-workers.

And it's certainly no way to begin a healthy flirting relationship.

So, Dr. Flirt and "The Etiquettes"—Emily P., Amy V. and Letitia B. advise against overdressing, using sex appeal and acting outside of your sex role (i.e., masculine females, feminine males) except at costume parties. You can flirt just fine wearing business clothes.

Remember: If you're not enjoying yourself, you're not flirting.

THE SHORT LIST OF OFFICE FLIRTING SCENARIOS

....

SCENARIO 1- The Old Line

ROLES: men = knights; women = the "weaker sex"

ACTIONS:

- Men mold themselves on the cowboy/John Wayne model. You may find them married to "the little woman." They may believe women look to them to "think for us both," or they may put women on pedestals, thinking of them as mysterious objects of desire. They assume women have "no head for" mechanical details, figures, etc.

- Men open doors, pull out chairs, give up their seats, help with coats, light cigarettes, place food orders, fetch drinks, pick up the tab, pump gas, etc., for women.

Warning: the Old Line may still exist in many places, particularly in organizations where pre- and early-1960s men have ascended to control positions or where corporate culture has not evolved since the 1960s. Some women may be comfortable with this situation, in which they are cast primarily in supportive roles. Those who are not so comfortable should be clear about the office culture before agreeing to take on projects or jobs there. If employed, you must be ready for the balanced diplomacy of compromise and assertiveness that this environment will require of you.

Beware of blatant problems. A woman I know was hired on at the U.S. office of an overseas company, where the managers left pornographic comics in the employee lounge. Not from U.S. culture, these managers had little respect for the opinions of women. So the offensive comics stayed, and my friend and other women employees quit. Everyone, at some time, may be faced with a question of whether the job is more important than their self-respect.

Old-line awareness also applies if you are a woman taking your car or any appliance in to be serviced. If you see photos of half-naked women hanging on the walls, you may not expect that your concerns will be fully addressed by the shop employees.

SCENARIO 2- The New Line

ROLES: men and women = teammates/competitors

ACTIONS:

- Equal partnership in business and marriage means mutual chivalry; whoever gets to the door first opens it; each person thinks for him- or herself; each helps with chairs, coats, ordering, drinks, gas-pumping, etc.; each picks up the tab.

The elder males of your workforce will be the more likely to help women with coats, pull out chairs, rise when women enter a room and give up their seats at meetings and on buses. Older women may expect and appreciate these flirtatious "common courtesies." But they may make younger women feel awkward.

If they bother you, speak privately with the male(s) in question, and ask that they let you do these things yourself. There's no reason you can't open the door or hold the coat for an older man, or "go Dutch" on bar and meal bills.

This doesn't mean chivalry is dead. It just means it's evolving.

FLIRT POWER

The workplace runs on information: promotions, demotions, job openings and cuts, departmental changes, company successes and problems, even personal items such as births and parties.

The more information you have, the better you'll operate in this environment. And *flirting* is the key.

Your warmth and friendliness can open doors to that information (to use for *good*, not for evil). Practice the First Rule Of Flirting (make 'em feel special), and people will return the favor to you.

For example, my mother the travel agent always delivers tickets to her clients in person. She depends on building friendships to win new business and keep current customers coming back for more.

One executive I know makes sure that every week, he wishes, "Good morning!" at least once to each of the 50-plus people who work for him. A salesman I know trades recipes with receptionists wherever he calls for business. A manager I know makes it a point to befriend people whom her officemates mark as "impossible." You never know when *anyone's* help or advice will come in handy.

Workplaces also run on respect for space. The space allotment tells you immediately what function each person has and how important each person is (including you) in the company hierarchy. Within each of these spaces, each person also has their own personal space you must respect.

Q: Can I use any of the Proven Flirting Techniques at work?

A: Yes. Use them all—in the elevator, the boardroom, the cafeteria, on voice-mail, E-Mail or FAX. But *only* with the mutual understanding, between you and your flirtee, that the purpose is to have fun.

To avoid peccadillos, I strongly advise you to follow:

DR. FLIRT'S OFFICIAL GUIDE TO WORKPLACE FLIRTING

- Have a good time spreading flirtatious cheer throughout your office(s).

- Only move in close to people you know and with whom you feel comfortable.

- Get permission before you touch or squeeze any body part of anybody.

- Enjoy the repartee and innuendo, but only with people you know, who agree this sort of banter is okay. Doing it with people you don't know is hunting, not flirting.

- If you receive no response to your flirtatious comment, drop it. Pursuing the person with more comments, just to get a reaction, is harassment.

- If you anticipate any question about your conduct, don't do it (see 7th Rule of Flirting).

Nobel Prize physicist Richard Feynman writes in his book, *Surely You're Joking, Mister Feynman* (Bantam), that his usual technique for meeting someone is just to go up and introduce himself. But in one situation, he wanted to meet a locksmith who had important information about office safes, and he knew the smith wouldn't give him the details unless he felt comfortable with Feynman. The physicist's technique is instructive for anybody who wants to do good workplace flirting.

First, Feynman learned where and what hours the locksmith worked. Then he just walked by the fellow's open door a few days in a row, to get the locksmith familiar with seeing him. Nothing more. The next few days, Feynman would say, "Hi" as he passed. Finally, the locksmith started saying "Hi" back. After a few weeks of this process, they started making short comments: "Hi! I see you're working pretty hard!"

"Yeah, pretty hard."

Then, a breakthrough: the locksmith invited Feynman for soup in the cafeteria. After that, they would meet for meals now and then, and talk about general things, such as solving problems with machines, and only after another week did Feynman get around to asking about office safes.

Remember, folks: flirting is for the long term.

Cheer and friendliness at the workplace are always acceptable. Sensual undertones and overtones carry danger, even if both parties are consenting adults. Office romances can breed innuendo and gossip that can lead to embarrassments and job problems.

THE "H" WORD

How to deal with sexual harassment is outside the scope of this book. But be advised: one person's flirt could be another person's come-on. Behavior we accept as appropriate from one person we may find inappropriate from another. Basically, harassment violates all rules of flirting.

So, "read" each situation. Use Feynman's careful example when approaching someone new. And follow the Official Guide to Workplace Flirting. These should keep you safe. When you flirt in the workplace, neither your ego, nor your future should be on the line.

Q: Is there any research about this stuff, Dr. Flirt?

A: Of course. Flirting research is a relatively new field, but crowds of people are exploring it. Most of the research takes place at colleges and universities, because that's where most of the researchers teach. But the results can often be applied everywhere.

For example, researchers at the University of South Alabama found that men and women tend to similarly interpret flirting actions of the opposite sex.

Three variables—place, type of comment and effort expended—affect perceptions of flirting. A person who puts forth some effort to initiate contact is often seen as flirtatious. So, you'll get more flirt mileage out of paying a compliment than asking for the time of day. Also, an interaction in a bar is more likely to be seen as flirtatious than one in a library.

A 1985 study of 200 randomly selected University of Missouri female students (Moore), found 52 separate behaviors by women that elicited male attention (many are contained in the Complete List in chapter 1). Women who "signal" to men are the ones most often approached by men.

A 1987 South Alabama study found that males were more likely than females to follow up a flirtation, and singles more likely than marrieds.

Singles, younger students or those in a lower class year or who had lower grades, were more likely to experience jealousy. The researchers suggested that decreased jealousy in older students may result from increased maturity and self-esteem.

Finally, there's a growing body of research on sexual harassment. Both men and women may view physical advances, propositions, sexist comments and undue attention as offensive, harassing or both, but which depends on the context of the action. Legal charges may result.

For further reading, I refer you to Bernard Asbell and Karen Wynn's readable book of behavior studies, *What They Know About You* (Random House). It contains more than you might ever want to know about yourself and everybody else.

FLIRTING AT SCHOOL

Unfortunately, you may need to worry about sexual harassment at school, too. But when there's a problem here, you can generally go to your teachers, big friends, counselors, principal or parents to get it resolved.

Q: Can I use the Proven Flirting Techniques at school?

A: Of course. In fact, there's more freedom to use them there, because the whole purpose of school is to create an atmosphere in which you can explore, experiment and play. That is another reason why most research, including flirting studies, is done at colleges and universities. In fact, in 1982, researchers did a school flirting study at Valparaiso University, in California. They found that three quarters of students surveyed believed flirting could raise a female student's grade. Half believed it could raise a male student's grade. Less than a quarter believed flirting could lower a grade. In spite of that, only 8 percent reported believing that their grades had been changed as a result of flirting.

The easiest ways to flirt at school are dropping books, smiling shyly, passing notes and shooting spitwads.

If you're more sophisticated, you can use most any technique from the Complete List. Remember your Fourth Rule of Flirting: Take everything one step at a time. Try this method:

If you're in class, you might check to see if you can make eye or other non-verbal contact with this person. If so, how often, and is it friendly? If it's friendly, find an excuse to "break the ice" and talk with the person about something harmless, such as what happened in class, what the assignments are or an upcoming school event.

If the conversation goes well, suggest this person join you in doing something you were already planning to do: go to the mall or your favorite burger place, a movie or event, or, as a last resort, study at home together under supervision. Studying is a great excuse to get together.

To avoid embarrassment, you want a simple reason for getting together that has nothing to do with being attracted to this person. That way, you can treat your behavior as just being friendly. You don't want to tip your hand before you see the other person likes you, too.

Whether you're an adult, teen or child, I caution that, if you find a flirting interest, take things one step at a time. I don't know how many men I've met who think, in this sexually pressured society of ours, that simple interest from a woman means a ticket to bed. It doesn't. It means she is curious to converse or do some innocent activity with the man, and learn more about him. That's why we flirt.

Q: How do I know if there's interest, Dr. Flirt?

A: There is interest if the person you approach *does* want to talk, dance, share a drink, go to a movie or event with you. There's also evidence of interest if they decline your invitation now, but suggest a get-together at another time. There is no interest if the person simply doesn't respond, or says "no" to anything now or later.

Q: Suppose my prospect is in a group. We dance and he/she goes back to the group. How do I go further?

A: Approach, excuse yourself and ask for another dance, or ask if he/she wants to join you for a beverage. If you can't get in edgewise, then hand the person a card with a note of what you want to do. It could be anything from dancing or meeting at that time, to meeting at another time in broad daylight, on neutral territory, at a time of mutual convenience.

Q: What if somebody starts flirting with my spouse/significant other (S/SO) at a party?

A: Depending on the circumstances, it could be flattering to have the person of your choice become an object of warm attention. To ascertain this, observe whether or not this attention appears to be innocent, and how your S/SO is reacting. If he or she is enjoying an innocent and spirited conversation, this may be an opportunity for you to meet someone new and start a friendship. If your S/SO is enjoying having someone "put a move" on them, this is a danger sign. If the S/SO is rejecting an advance, be relieved they are indicating no interest, and be prepared to come to the rescue.

Conversely, if you are flirting with someone, and they turn out to be somebody's S/SO, just include the "other" in any flirting invitation you make. The objective here is to make friends. Remember?

Q: Are there ways I should never open a conversation?

A: Yes. *Never* say:

- Is that your real hair?

- Lemme see your tan line.

- I wanna meet you honey. I don't mean M-E-E-T. I mean M-E-A-T.

- Hey, baby!

- What is the love we feel for each other?

- How many men/women have you slept with?

- Would you like to see my etchings? (unless you are an etchings artist, or are known for your collection)

- I'm writing a book about flirting.

- When's the baby due? or How long have you been pregnant? (particularly if this female is large and you don't know the reason).

- Do you like knives/guns/kinky stuff?

- If I told you you have gorgeous body, would you hold it against me?

- What's your momma feed you to make you look so fine?

- I bet I can out-drink you!

- Your place or mine?

- You remind me of a woman/man I used to date.

- Do you really eat that junk?

Also, avoid starting with a probing question, such as, "How do you keep your kids off drugs?" or, "Where'd you get the money for these fine clothes?" or, "So what do you do for a living?"

Better to start with "What kinds of things do you enjoy doing?" After living many years on the east and west coasts, I've deciphered this apparent difference between East and West Coast conversations. Eastern questions are usually related to work and achievements; Western questions relate to quality of life.

There are flirting differences between North and South, too. A Georgia friend of mine says that pronouncing eloquent titles and compliments is a way of life in the South, and you'd better learn flirting if you want to do business there.

This courtly behavior is also practiced on the floors of the U.S. Senate and House of Representatives. And it is a reason why it's so entertaining to read Southern writers.

"Charm," says my friend, "is more important than intelligence."

Q: Are there ways I should always open a conversation?

A: There's no one opening line that always works. I do hear some good ones, such as, "Didn't we go to kindergarten together?" But basically, if you follow the suggestions in Flirt Conversation 101 and 102, you'll be off to a flying start.

The element of surprise is fun, too. If you can learn something about your intended flirt person, and surprise them with that fact, they'll usually enjoy it: "I didn't know you were a triathaloner!" or "You know, we're neighbors!"

There are things you should never do, too.

A woman journalist friend of mine was covering a convention once, wearing her "Press" badge, and some guy came up and pressed it. Don't do that, friends.

Q: How do I keep people from thinking I'm going too far?

A: Tell them. We flirters go into flirting assuming we are attractive to our prospective flirtees. We believe they can't resist responding, and will want to spend their time being playful with us. This isn't necessarily true. If you are only out to flirt, or if you have a purpose beyond flirting, you must let the person know that, and you must get that same information from them, to avoid misunderstandings.

After high school, there's really nowhere adults are chaperoned. So, we become responsible for setting our own rules and boundaries for each interaction as we go along. Knowing how to act is easy where spaces are clearly defined, such as on the telephone, at a counter, or in line for a movie or shopping. But you'll have to be more specific at work, in a bar, public place, dance or party.

I must admit, there are ambiguous situations, too.

Q: Suppose in a bar, club or outdoors, I see someone wearing suggestive clothing. Are they hunting? Do they want to be approached and fondled?

A: No. Folks, this is a lose-lose situation. How someone dresses is their business. Even if you think they "look like they're asking for it," stay away. Noboby is "asking for it," and no bouncer, cop or court in America will accept that excuse as a reason for you to make unwelcome sexual advances.

Unfortunately, it's natural for us in America to get the impression that everyone is a potential sex object. Every day, we are bombarded with sexual messages in our media, conveyed primarily by people who wear tight-fitting clothes.

I was out bicycling once and I saw a woman who wore a hot pink Spandex body suit, riding a hot pink ten-speed bike. I assumed she wanted to be noticed, so I said hello. She sprinted away from me. I have no idea what was on that woman's mind.

And that's my point. We can't know what motivates someone to dress the way they do. As long as they don't violate conventions, such as wearing lingerie or boxer shorts to work, they're fine. Admire their taste and physiques, but respect their privacy.

If you feel compelled to approach such a person anyway, you find them irresistibly magnetic, or you shiver at their novelty, then read the situation and see what this person is doing. If they appear approachable, open with something truthful, such as, "I'd like to meet the real you in somewhere other than this unreal place." Your objective is to break through their "dressed up" persona, to the real human inside. However, this man or woman may not want anyone to know the real person inside, which means you and everybody else may just be out of luck this time.

And if you meet them another time in broad daylight, they may not look attractive at all. A 1979 study done in country and western bars found that men and women look more and more attractive to each other as the evening wears on. So beware.

7
• • • • •

REAL LIFE FLIRTING OPTIONS AND CREATIVE DATING

Well, we've come a long way together, and now Dr. Flirt will open his diaries to you. Yes friends, we know each other well enough to have established some trust. And in that spirit, I can at last reveal to you these private notes from years of flirting and Creative Dating.

FLIRTING OPTIONS DIARY

FOR SHY PEOPLE: Are you afraid to talk to anyone, especially in a public situation (party, bar, or at work)? Write a note.

Option 1: Say your voice is not working very well, but you'd sure like to talk quietly. Have someone carry the note for you. When your person looks up, wave plaintively, and gesture for them to join you.

Option 2: Say your voice isn't working well, and ask what this person thinks about some subject you want to talk about. Again, get someone to take the note over for you, but this time don't reveal who you are. If your prospect is intrigued, tell your messenger to have them write back. After you have exchanged a few notes, you may reveal yourself.

Option 3: Instead of sending someone a drink (sometimes people think that's a "pick-up" technique), send them an appetizer, one corn chip, or a bag of peanuts—something silly to tease them a little before revealing it was you.

Option 4: Make a request. Tell the person you are lost or new in town, and want advice. Or ask for help: "Will you do this for me? You do it so much better."

Option 5: Find a greeting card with a message that conveys your sense of humor, write your request in it and send it to your prospect (you need a messenger, or their address and a stamp). If they call back and say, "I didn't get the joke," you'll know something important about them. Likewise if they say, "That was the funniest card I've ever seen!"

FOR EVERYBODY: Use a prop. This "telegraphs" your area of interest to other people, and attracts those with similar interests.

Option 1: Borrow somebody's dog for a walk, or somebody's baby. See what kinds of people you meet.

Option 2: Are you a science fiction nut? A birdwatcher? An art or movie buff? Bring a book to a café or party, plop yourself down and start reading, holding up the book so others can see the cover. If nobody approaches, at least you'll get some reading done. If people do approach, you've made contact.

Option 3: Wear a T-shirt printed with a cause you believe in or place you love to visit, a plain or electric flashing button or jewelry, or some other distinctive clothing. It all invites comment, and comments invite responses from you.

Option 4: Practice a skill, such as juggling, music, dancing, whittling or origami. Sit down in a bar with a sketch pad and draw, and see how people start asking for portraits and offering to buy you drinks.

Option 5: Carry a camera. People will want to know what you're shooting pictures of.

Option 6: Go compliment your prospect on something (hair, jewelry, jacket, how they carry themselves or go ask a question, "What are you reading? I've been watching you, and guessed you were a fireman. Are you?")

Option 7: Enter a room with authority. Stand tall there, framed in the doorway, until a few heads turn, then saunter in about your business. You'll convey the impression you're important. That's good for points.

Option 8: Get a vanity license plate; I saw one on a Dallas Corvette: ME JANE; on a London Rolls Royce: EGO; on a New York Mercedes: MEIN; on a Seattle 4x4: BOYTOY. People ask about this stuff.

As you can see, there are tons of ideas for the approach, after you're done winking, arching your eyebrows, tipping your hat, raising your glass and smiling to catch their attention.

You can even flirt with several people at once. When two jovial female friends of mine were in Chicago a while back, they wanted to see the Second City comedy troupe, but all the tickets were sold out.

They went to the saloon downstairs and asked the bartender how they could get in. He pointed out two fellows who worked in the show, and suggested asking them.

My friend walked up to them and declared, "Hey, I hate oysters, but I'll eat three on the half shell if you can get us tickets to this show." They struck up a conversation, ended up with tickets, saw the show and then all went out afterward.

CREATIVE DATING

As you can see from the Second City example, what begins as friendly flirting can turn into an actual date. With your self-confidence and playfulness, you have won yourself a rendezvous with some delightful person.

Now what?

Let's start by *not* calling it a "date." That word has too much high school baggage attached to it.

So, forget all that stuff. Let's create something new—a CreativeDate.

This is not your standard movie and dinner. Although, if you spend most of your time running marathons and drinking liquid meals, then dinner and a movie *would* be a CreativeDate (or CD) for you.

CreativeDates don't have to just be with a new romantic interest, by the way. Parents can do them with children, married couples can do them, best friends can do them, you can take your grandmother on one. In fact, Dr. Flirt was involved in one for a bachelor party recently. Instead of the standard party, the guys took the groom to the local old folks' home, where we were set up with coffee, cookies and several of the old women, to talk about their wedding days and marriages. They were delighted to see so many handsome young men, and we learned a lot about life.

The CreativeDate prompts people to think, innovate and enjoy.

There's some question about who invented CreativeDating. Back in 1982, Edna Kellman and Bruce M. Green were innovating and practicing it at Brandeis-Bardin Institute in Southern California. Doug Fields and Todd Temple, however, were the first to write a book about it, *Creative Dating* (Oliver-Nelson) in 1986.

I lean toward Edna and Bruce because they are friends of mine and Edna, who is now my wife, contributed to writing this section of the book. In fact, when we first met at a party several years ago, I asked her, "Do you date?" She replied, "No. I CreativeDate." We hit it off. The rest is history.

But I digress. If you have been successfully flirting with this object of your desire, you are about to be alone with them for the first time. You want it to be very comfortable for both of you. None of this taking forever to decide on the "right" restaurant, so you can spend the evening watching each other eat. And you don't want to spend the time worrying whether you got a poppyseed stuck in your teeth. Neither do you want to just sit silently with this stranger in a dark room, watching a film run. You could do that at home.

So, what do you do?

Something creative, of course. Something that gives you a chance to interact with this person, learn who they are and start building a friendship. Just as you had to find something in common to begin your flirting, now find an *activity* you can *do* in common, that will be fun, and a little different.

You learn more about people from their actions than their talk. Actions speak louder than words.

CREATE A SURPRISE

You invite your person by phone, or by written invitation, telling them only how to dress for the occasion, and when to be ready for you to pick them up.

If your person doesn't deal well with surprises, that tells you something about their ability to be spontaneous. It also tells you something if they've never been outdoors without a necktie, or they don't own a pair of comfortable shoes. It also tells you something if they retaliate before your date by sending you flowers, or finding some other way to surprise you.

We recommend your first CD be on a weekend during the day (the zoo, a street fair, a drive to a favorite antique shop, the children's museum, the state fair) and that it allows you the chance to be a child. As author Tom Robbins says, "It's never too late to have a happy childhood." CreativeDates are most successful when they encourage laughter.

If you don't feel comfortable being spontaneous, you can be innovative anyway. Peg the CD to the season: visit an arboretum in spring when everything blooms; at Christmas hit Williamsburg or go snorkeling in the Caribbean. (One visit to Williamsburg, I was roped into a lawn bowling tournament, and ended up bowling the winning ball for my team!) Go for a walk the first day the snow falls, take a hot-air balloon ride the first day of summer. Throw a Solstice party at sunrise, or take afternoon tea at a fancy hotel.

You can peg your CD to times of day. Get to a bakery in the middle of the night as the fresh bread comes out, and have a feast with some cheese and wine, or do a picnic at sunrise on a hill or monument that faces east. One Sunday, visit a church with a great gospel choir. Have a tea ceremony at sunset.

Use community resources. You can watch videos and movies free at your local library or college, as well as hear lectures and see concerts at reduced rates. Run the Par/Health Course at your local park, then go eat at a health food restaurant. Millions of you are lucky enough to live in cities with ferry boats. These are great CreativeDate machines.

Devote a day to community service, delivering goods to shut-ins, working at a soup kitchen or shelter or doorbelling to get signatures for a cause in which you believe.

There's no better way than a CD to test whether or not the person who interests you shares your interests.

CD (CREATIVEDATE) DIARY: KEEP IT SIMPLE

Option 1: Take a walk. It's informal, cheap and low pressure. No need to find the "right" restaurant or movie. You can talk and get to know one another, without being forced to have constant eye contact. You ease into it, shyly. Walk around a lake, down a trail or take an urban hike and window-shop. The passing scenery gives you tons of things to discuss. Stop for food at a hot dog stand or a grocery store. Get to know this person by what he/she says, chooses to eat and spend, and by what side-trips he/she suggests.

Option 2: A picnic in some unusual place—on top of a building, on a ferry-boat, on a tailgate at the polo grounds. Or a gourmet picnic in a rustic set-ting—in the woods, on a farm, at a fish ladder. If it's raining out, make the picnic on your floor. If you do the ferryboat, have dessert at the far landing, say, a bakery over there. Then when someone asks you, "How was your first date?" You can say, "Awesome! We walked on water."

Option 3: Do a theme. Got tickets to a concert? Send your date an unmarked cassette of the music or group a week before you go. Got tickets to a show? Send the book. Planning a game of putt-putt golf? Have someone deliver a golf ball with a note saying, "See you on Thursday..." Going to an art exhibit or a museum? Send a postcard with one of the paintings or art pieces on it.

Option 4: Do spontaneous things inside the date. Go to a bookstore and each agree to purchase one children's book for the other person. Read to each other out loud. Or, split up and buy each other some exotic item at a candy store. Go to a hat store and try on several hats each.

Option 5: Attend a one-night art class or cooking class together at an exper-imental college. One of my students brought his first date to my flirting class.

Option 6: Have your friends help. Ask them to make spaghetti and salad and ice cream, then take it to your CreativeDate's place for dinner. You'll know if this person is a "fit" in your life, if they get along with your friends. To make it more interesting, have the four of you eat dinner with only aprons and surgical gloves, or chopsticks.

Option 7: Add a stipulation to make things interesting. For example, have the whole CD involve no money. Or have it center around making the world a better place to live. Or make it involve chocolate, no matter what.

All of these options simply continue your initial flirting that started the whole thing off. And they help give you a clear idea who your prospect is, and they give your prospect a clear idea who you are. If you are successful this first time, next time it will be your CreativeDate's turn to plan things.

The structure is up to you. Putting your respective energies into CreativeDates will take a lot of pressure off the first few dates, and spice things up as time goes on.

The great thing about a CreativeDate is, if things falls apart, it's okay. That's just part of the creativity. You can make things up as you go along, or change things in the middle and explain that's how you'd planned it all along. Whether it works or not, you learn a lot—about yourself, about your date and about the activity.

The No-Defect Law of Flirting applies to CreativeDating, too: You never really make a mistake. You just provide yourself a learning experience to have more fun next time.

THE RULES OF FLIRTING

···

THE FIRST RULE OF FLIRTING
Make yourself, and somebody else, feel special.

THE SECOND RULE OF FLIRTING
Flirt where you're comfortable. Flirt who you are.

THE THIRD RULE OF FLIRTING
Keep your sense of humor. Don't take yourself too seriously.

THE FOURTH RULE OF FLIRTING
Take everything one step at a time.

THE FIFTH RULE OF FLIRTING
Approach your prospect immediately. Do not wait.

THE SIXTH RULE OF FLIRTING
When you flirt, create movement. A gentle chase.

THE SEVENTH RULE OF FLIRTING
"Read" the person and situation where you want to flirt.

Refer to p. 70 for Dr. Flirt's Official Guide to Workplace Flirting

BIBLIOGRAPHY

Future Shock, Alvin Toffler; Bantam, New York: 1970.

For Yourself: The Fulfillment of Female Sexuality, Lonnie Garfield Barbach; Signet, New York: 1975.

Male Sexuality, Bernie Zilbergeld Ph.D.; Bantam Books, New York: 1978.

Love, Sex and Marriage Through the Ages, Bernard Murstein; Springer, New York: 1974.

The Road Less Traveled, M. Scott Peck, MD; Touchstone/Simon & Schuster, New York: 1978.

How to Make a Man Fall in Love with You, Tracy Cabot Ph.D.; Dell Publishing, New York: 1984.

How to Get Angry Without Feeling Guilty, Adelaide Bry, New American Library/Dutton, New York: 1986.

You Just Don't Understand, Deborah Tannen, Ph.D.; Ballantine Books, New York: 1990.

What They Know About You, Bernard Asbell with Karen Wynn; Random House, New York: 1991.

Body Language, Julius Fast; Simon & Schuster Pocket Books, New York: 1970.

Face Language, Robert Whiteside, Simon & Schuster Pocket Books: 1974.

Subtext, Julius Fast; Viking, New York: 1991

Embarassment in America, a work in progress by Edward Gross Ph.D., University of Washington Dept. of Sociology

The Secret Language of Success, David Lewis, Carroll & Graf Publishers, Inc., New York: 1989.

Messages, the Communications Skills Book, McKay, Davis & Fanning; New Harbinger Publications, Oakland, CA, 1987.

Marci's Secret Book of Flirting, Jan Gelman; Knopf, New York: 1990.

The Fine Art of Flirting, Joyce Jillson; Simon & Schuster Fireside Books, 1984.

Sunday New York Times Japan Trade Advertising Supplement, Bill Totten, March 24, 1991.

Surely You're Joking, Mister Feynman, Richard Feynman; Bantam, New York: 1985.

STUDIES

"Sex Differences in Factors of Romantic Attraction," Jeffrey Nevid, St. John's University, 1984.

"Courtship in the Personals Column: The Influence of Gender and Sexual Orientation," Kay Deaux and Randel Hanna, 1984, Purdue University.

"The Relationship of Weight, the Self Perception of Weight and Self Esteem With Courtship Behavior," David Kallen and Andrea Doughty, 1984, Michigan State University.

"Cognitive Structure of Sexual Harassment: Implications for University Policy," Steven C. and Janet S. Padgitt, 1986, Iowa State University.

"Flirting Between College Students and Faculty," David Rowland, Larry Crisler and Donna Cox, 1982, Valparaiso University.

"Non-Verbal Courtship Patterns in Women: Context and Consequences," Monica Moore, 1985, University of Missouri.

"Self-Report Measures of Behavioral Attributions Related to Interpersonal Flirtation Situations," Jerrold Downey and William Vitulli, 1987, University of South Alabama.

"The Effects of Place, Type of Comment, and Effort Expended on the Perception of Flirtation," March, 1991, *Journal of Social Behavior and Personality*.

"Psycholological Aspects of the Male-Female Relationship," Bruno Rhyner, 1984, Kyoto University.

"Competitive vs. Non-Competitive Styles: Which Is Most Valued in Courtship?" Mary Laner, 1986, Arizona State University.

"Jealousy and Irrationality in Love," David Lester, George Deluca, William Hellinghausen and David Scribner, 1985, Stockton State College (California).

"Don't the Girls Get Prettier at Closing Time: A Country and Western Application to Psychology." Pannebaker, J.W., et al, Personality and Social Psychology, 1979, v.5, p. 122.

ABOUT THE AUTHOR

Marty Westerman, known as "Dr. Flirt" to his nationwide audience, is a lifelong flirt who believes that flirting is a healthy way to bring out the playful side in everybody. He suggests you use flirting to meet new friends or that "special" someone; to give mundane chats an exciting twist; or just to enjoy yourself on the spur of the moment.

During more than a quarter century of learning and laughing, he has developed a unique method of teaching others the tricks of the trade while having fun. He lost his bachelor's in flirting when he got married, but his lovely wife Edna has awarded him a master's, and together they are proof that, single or married, flirting enables each of us to create a little romance in our daily lives.

photo by Eddie Westerman

He makes his home in Seattle, Washington with his wife, Eddie,
their son, Max, their goldfish Barney Google
and their mechanical dog, Life.